PRAISE FOR
Memoir of Mourning

I read *Memoir of Mourning* without stopping. When I did, tears welled up—it is written so beautifully, with such communication and feeling. It is a continuous poem, so easy to read. It reminded me of years ago when I read the impressive novel, *Kamouraska*— written by the accomplished Québécoise author of fiction, poetry and drama, Anne Hébert.

This well-constructed volume is written with such sensitivity— ability to feel, express and share—combining simple plain words with clarity to produce strong imagery. She touchingly tells us stories from her own and her mother's life to provide insights into the process of healing, remembering and the importance of the present, family and friends.

Importantly, Chowaniec also points out the failings of the acute care medical system in communicating with family to assist in understanding and dealing with illness and death—calling for physicians to have increased empathy, knowledge of palliative care and the ability to explain, comfort and guide.

It is a must-read for both doctors in training and those in established practice.

—Mary Morris, MD, PhD, FRCP, Adjunct Professor, Faculty of Medicine, University of Ottawa

This book becomes everywoman's story as the author probes and shares the meaning of death. Ultimately, the author finds new life in a horsehair star, an open ear, silver threaded through a green silk shawl.

—Maggie Kast, author of *The Crack between the Worlds: A Dancer's Memoir of Loss, Faith and Family*

Your writing is thoughtful, sensitive and creative. It is a great accomplishment. The poetry is poignant and very visual. Reading your poems and text has caused me to reflect on the delight that my own mother is and how lucky I am to have her in my life.

Your honesty is so helpful when we reach that point when we need to process our grief and loss.

—Barb Gamble, artist

I think *Memoir of Mourning* provides tremendous solace. The author is open and honest about her feelings and we want to listen to what she tells us. We find it hard to talk about death and mourning. We avert our eyes from the subject. Death and our own mortality terrify us!

Claudia speaks of the value of remembering to remember, especially all the joyful celebrations. Reading this has made me decide to go back into my own life and reinstate the celebratory things.

—Ilina Straberg, writer, editor and producer

Your voice is so authentic—I feel I'm right there with you. The feelings you describe are still so raw inside me even after all these years. They hurt, but they are so precious. I think of my mother every day.

—Sandra O'Neill Page, actor, playwright, producer

All in all, a moving and telling story. I'm no expert on book marketing but it should find a hungry readership.

—Dr. Rob Cushman, Senior Medical Advisor at Health Canada

Memoir of Mourning raises a number of poignant human issues that surround the death of a parent—the loss itself, the transition of the adult child from the younger generation to the older generation, and the painful learning of what the process of death entails. It also highlights the way our contemporary North American culture has allowed traditional rituals of grief and mourning to fall into disuse. As Claudia looks at the rituals of other cultures, she gives us a vivid and moving description of a lantern-lit procession on All Souls night—*La Dia de los Muertos*—in San Francisco's Mission District.

Most of us will face the issues raised in this book. They are worth reading and thinking about.

 —Jean Van Loon, author and poet

Every journey is expected to have some hardships and some enlightenment, especially a journey of grief. This memoir is no exception, except that this journey feels real, as if you were taking it yourself with a kindly mentor at your side. In your journey, you might have changed the mother to another relative or friend, but most of the feelings remain the same. The mentor helps to soften somewhat the burden of grief by examining it in its many parts and phases. The examination leads to an unraveling to expose deeper feelings, such as guilt, which is more predominantly felt by women. Most of us have more experience dealing with guilt than with loss. The brightness that lightens the journey is through becoming intimately acquainted with a loving mother and her relationship with her loving daughter.

 —Elizabeth Diem, RN, PhD, community nursing education consultant, retired from University of Ottawa, School of Nursing

MEMOIR

OF

MOURNING

Journey through
Grief and Loss
to Renewal

MEMOIR

OF

MOURNING

Journey through
Grief and Loss
to Renewal

CLAUDIA CHOWANIEC

AMIGA PRESS   OTTAWA CANADA

The poem "Thanksgiving Day" was originally published in the *Queen's Quarterly*, Queen's University, Kingston, Ontario, Autumn 2012.

Library and Archives Canada Cataloguing in Publication

Chowaniec, Claudia, 1949-, author
    Memoir of mourning : journey through grief and loss to renewal / Claudia Chowaniec.

Issued in print and electronic formats.
ISBN 978-0-9919620-0-6 (pbk.).--ISBN 978-0-9919620-2-0 (print on demand).--ISBN 978-0-9919620-1-3 (pdf)

    1. Grief. 2. Bereavement--Psychological aspects. 3. Loss (Psychology). 4. Mothers--Death--Psychological aspects. 5. Chowaniec, Claudia, 1949-. I. Title.

BF575.G7C52 3013   155.9'37092   C2013-902749-1
                                               C2013-902750-5

For more information please contact:
  Claudia Chowaniec
  www.MemoirofMourning.com

A portion of the net proceeds benefits the Hospice at May Court.

Cover design and photo by Keef Ward

Printed in USA

To my dearest family
We share our love and our loss of
Mom/Oma and are comforted by her
ongoing spiritual presence.

I hope
sharing my stories
will help
comfort you
in your deep sorrow and
bring you solace.

Your journey
My journey
I would like to share this with you
I am certain we are not alone.

Contents

Introduction:
A Personal Message to the Reader

In *Memoir of Mourning*, I'm writing about my mother's death, my immense sorrow and loneliness after her passing and my gradual recognition, now almost four years later, that I have come to a new, more hopeful place in my life. I accept that the deep sadness will always be there. But what we shared, all the happy memories, are there too. I'm making progress on my journey to a deeper understanding of death and life, joy and sorrow, and I'm learning that time does heal—eventually.

You may already have gone through this difficult life passage or you may have yet to experience it. Caring for our aging parents, being with them as they are dying, and mourning their loss, have an impact on our own inner life and our perception of ourselves as adults. But it isn't just our parents that we're losing. Spouse, colleague, neighbor, so many of our friends are passing on. Ten thousand baby boomers are turning sixty-five every day for the next decade. We all expect to live another quarter of a century at least. Coping with our loved ones' end of life and dealing with our own mortality are profound challenges that we're facing.

Memoir of Mourning is based on memories and excerpts from the journal I began before Mom's death. I scribbled down my thoughts—raw, intense and immediate—on what was happening in the hospital as I tried to communicate with the medical team, *Is Mom dying?* I recorded the end-of-life decisions I struggled to make, when out of the blue the doctors told me they were discharging Mom because there was nothing more they could do for her and she needed palliative care. The journal became the only witness to my anxious bedside vigil, *What will death be like?* as I watched her breathe, one breath, then another, and then no breath at all.

My mother died on her ninety-fourth birthday in early spring and I continued journaling as my way of dealing with my grief. Writing things down has always been easier for me than saying them, so my journaling brought me some comfort.

The book is divided into three parts: "Dying and Death," "Mourning Mom" and "Journey toward Renewal." I have braided together three distinct strands in the weave of my story: the narrative of my personal experiences leading up to Mom's death, mourning, and moving on; poems to illuminate internal reflections in contrast with my outward persona; and snippets of research material and quotes from books about death and grieving.

As I was writing *Memoir of Mourning*, I came to realize what a relief it was for me to describe what I was going through and to share my experiences.

I look forward to continuing our conversations through my blog: www.SharingGrief.com and website: www.MemoirOfMourning.com.

I hope that sharing my story helps guide you through your deep sorrow and brings you solace.

Claudia Chowaniec
Ottawa, Canada
February 20, 2013

Prologue

My dearest daughter
I want to be free
I want to go home
I do not want
Anything here
Nothing
No thing
Please leave me alone
Tell them to leave me alone
I want to be alone
All by myself
I'm restless
I'm just so restless
Is it spring fever?
Is it still spring?
I want to go away
Far away
Over the hills
Far away
I want to be free
I want to go home
Home
Nowhere else
But home.
I want to go home.

Part 1

Dying and Death

1

Last Sunday evening at the retirement home where Mom had been living for the past nine years, she choked on her food while they were feeding her supper. She coughed and coughed. She could hardly catch her breath. They rushed her to emergency at our local hospital a few blocks away.

Wake up, Mom. Wake up. Do you know I'm here? Please open your eyes.

I stooped over the bedside railing whispering anxiously. Five days have passed since they brought her here and I've only just arrived. It was close to midnight and her room was dark except for a dim nightlight. I reached out to stroke her cheek, grasp her hand, get her attention. I wanted to shake her. Make her wake up.

Speak to me. Please speak to me. I raised my voice. Can you hear me? We'll get through this all right just as we have every other time you've been sick. It's okay. I'm here now. I'll look after you.

She lay quite still. Eyes closed. The intravenous line for the antibiotics looped to her arm. Bruised purple. White sheet pulled tight across the blue hospital gown. Pink swabs on the night table to moisten her lips. Tape to hold the IV line in place. Clear plastic water cup. Bright red tulip.

What should I do? I cranked up the pillow end of her bed. I tried to feed her a few spoons of the yogurt I'd brought. She didn't open her eyes. She didn't swallow and the yogurt dribbled from the corners of her mouth. I dabbed her lips. I ate the rest. I was so hungry but I didn't want to leave her to go back down to the hospital cafeteria. I was afraid she might wake up and not find me here. I'd already let her down.

I was not here when all this happened. Mom choking on her food. Mom rushed to emergency. I was away on holidays in the Caribbean enjoying the soothing heat of a mid-March winter escape. My husband is no "beach bunny" and he'd never liked the water, so I went with friends. We were having a great time, snorkeling, splashing in the waves, dancing under the stars, rum cocktails, glad to be away.

I'd been gone a day or two when I called home to ask about Mom. How is she? Does she miss me? Whenever I traveled, I left notes for Mom's caregivers, telling them where I was going and how long I'd be away. Mom was starting to forget things. She worried if I didn't keep our routine.

My husband told me what happened. All I could think of was I hadn't kept our routine.

He said, Your mother's in the hospital on antibiotics for pneumonia. But no need to rush home. Nothing you can do for her here. I've been to see her. And so has your brother.

She's delirious. She calls out. Her words are incomprehensible. I think she's speaking Dutch. I can't understand what she's saying. No one can.

Are you sure? I questioned him. I should come right home. I should be there to comfort her. She'll expect me to be there for her.

No really. My husband reassured me. Nothing you can do for her.

I stayed on for a few more days with my friends at the holiday resort. I felt guilty, but I was enjoying myself escaping for a while.

Now I was finally here five days after Mom had been taken to the hospital. The plane was late. A snowstorm. Unpredictable March. My husband picked me up at the airport. I was so excited to tell him about my trip. I hopped into the car. Still wearing my sneakers.

I'm taking you straight to the hospital, he said. Your mother might not make it through the night.

What? You told me I didn't need to come home early. Now you're saying she might die. I don't understand. How can this be?

We pulled up at the hospital entrance. I got out of the car. The lights were too bright. The air too cold. I'd been away, in the sun, in the heat. Now I was here. In shock. Angry too. Why didn't he tell me?

Admissions gave me directions to Mom's room. Down the long gray-green corridors. I found her alone in a darkened room. Only the nightlight on. Shadowy. Eyes closed.

I reached out to hold her hands. Mom. Mom. I'm here now.

A nurse came into the room. She must have seen me pass the nursing station.

She's been waiting for you, the nurse told me. She lies awake all night staring, eyes wide open.

Can I stay here? Can I spend the night? What should I do? I asked her. I was tired and hungry. I couldn't think straight. I wanted her to tell me.

I'll bring you a pillow for the chair by her bed. You can get some water or juice from the fridge in our little kitchen down the hall.

Thank you, I said, and settled down beside Mom.

Mom had been here in this hospital nine years ago. She'd had a stroke. They told me she wouldn't pull through. They told me to sign a do not resuscitate (DNR) form and to call her pastor.

I signed the form, but I didn't believe them. I sat by her bed, hour after hour, sometimes crying, sometimes reciting poems she had taught me, sometimes reading stories from her favorite religious books, which I'd picked up from the shelf in her room at the retirement home. For at least a week, maybe even ten days, she didn't move, didn't say a word. Then one day she just woke up. I was sitting there by her bed waiting. She smiled at me and reached out to hold my hand.

She revived slowly. She didn't fully recover. But she learned how to use a knife, fork and spoon again, hold a cup and stand on her own. She even walked short distances with a walker.

She was determined to get better.

She told me months later she knew I was there all that time even when she seemed to be in a coma. So I decided that's what I had to do now. I pushed down the side railings on the hospital bed. I leaned across to hold her hands and I began talking to her. I told her about my trip. She always liked to hear my travel stories. I prayed out loud. I recited all the poems I could think of. She didn't respond. I asked myself, Will it work this time? Or have I come too late? I was only away for a few days. She couldn't be dying because of that.

A few hours later I woke up cold and stiff. I'd fallen asleep in the hard gray leatherette armchair the nurse had placed beside Mom's bed for me. I wanted to go home. I stood, stretched and walked to the window. A wintry view of the adjacent hospital buildings. Still dark outside. Not quite dawn.

I called my husband. I felt confused. Angry too. Why didn't you tell me to come home immediately when they took Mom to emergency? I wanted to scream at him. Instead I whispered into my cell phone, She's sleeping quietly.

How is she? he asked.

I don't know. Nothing much to tell. She didn't open her eyes. She didn't squeeze my hand. She has an IV. She's being treated with antibiotics for pneumonia. I'm sure she'll get better, I said, desperately wanting to believe that. She's been in the hospital so many times before and she always gets better. I'm coming home now.

I needed to go home. Suddenly it was all I could think about. I hurried down the night-darkened hallway. It was quiet except for an occasional cry, someone calling out. I passed the nursing station, a brightly lit oasis in the surrounding gloom. The night nurse was still there, the one who brought me the pillow, the one who said Mom had been waiting for me for days. She made my guilt so much worse.

We made it through the night, I told her. As if I'd somehow single-handedly kept Mom alive. I'm sure she'll get better. I'm sure she knows I'm here now. I'll be back in a few hours. I'd like to speak with the doctor.

I went down in the elevator to the main entrance. I stepped out into icy winter and waved over a waiting taxi. The sun glowed orange, pink, gold, over the snowy field across the road from the hospital. I remembered when our eldest was born here thirty years ago. I held her in my arms that long ago dawn and watched the sun rise over the same field ripe with cornstalks then. The silver sliver moon hung barely visible in the slowly brightening sky. The big spruce beside the front door sheltered dozens of birds flitting in and out of the branches. A bright red cardinal called out, the notes still familiar from last fall. The first day of spring.

I returned to the hospital a few hours later. It was now day six since Mom had been brought here. I had spoken with my brother but the doctors hadn't given him any clear details either about Mom's condition. I sat down by her bed waiting, watching her breathe, one breath, then another.

A nurse came in. How is Mom? Will she get better? I asked anxiously. She offered comforting words, but no direct answer. The doctor will be along shortly, she assured me. She adjusted Mom's pillows. Changed the IV bag. Asked me about myself. She'd already met my brother and my husband. Where've you been? she asked. Nice tan. More guilt. I told her about being away on holidays. I told her about our family.

We have two grown-up daughters. My husband is away a lot at meetings and conferences. I work full-time. Sometimes it feels like much more than full-time, but I do have some flexibility in how I schedule my day, and that helps. I run my own management consulting practice so I can work nights and weekends to make up for the time I'll be here with Mom. I'm grateful for that, I told her.

What is Mom's diagnosis?

She's being treated with antibiotics for pneumonia.

Does she have pneumonia?

I don't know. The doctors haven't made that clear.

I settled down beside Mom's bed to wait for the doctor. Finally there he was. He strode into the room. He picked up Mom's chart. He checked her vital signs. He was young and brisk and impatient.

How's Mom doing? What's her diagnosis? Is she going to get better? Is she going to die?

She has pneumonia. We don't know yet if the antibiotic will be effective. But she's not actively dying, he said.

Claudia Chowaniec

What does that mean? Not actively dying, I asked hesitantly.

Not actively dying I thought. Meaningless words. Infuriating. I wanted to scream, but I couldn't do that. Much too reserved. Overly polite. In awe of the doctor. I wanted him to tell me how she was doing. I needed him to be direct and factual.

What's likely to happen next? Is she going to get better? Is she going to die? Why won't you tell me?

And, in the midst of my fear of the unknown, of what death would be like, I was angry and frustrated.

Is Mom dying?
Tears, endless tears.
Yours. Mine.
Endless tears.
Are you dying Mom?
How can I bear to lose you?
What are you feeling?
What are you thinking?
You haven't said a word to me
since they brought you here.
And we always share everything.

Does it hurt Mom?
Does dying hurt?
I'm so afraid of you dying.
I wish you'd speak to me.
Please tell me.
How are you feeling?
How can I help you?

Please tell me.

Why are you dying?
Don't you want to keep living?
Why won't you fight this?
You love life so much.
I love you so much.
You can't go
and leave me.

I don't know anything
about dying and death.
Help me understand.

Am I refusing to see the truth? I asked myself. No one is giving me the information I need—directly, honestly, openly—to help me begin to come to terms with this reality. I guess I know the truth somewhere deep inside, but I cannot confront it. I cannot let her go. Not yet.

After the doctor left I sat down again in that uncomfortable gray leatherette chair beside Mom's hospital bed waiting patiently for her to wake up and recognize me. Memories of all the times we had shared washed over me.

2

For the past nine years Mom had been settled in a small, sunny room at the retirement home just down the street from where my husband and I live. My brother and his wife are also close by. I'm four years older than he is. We each have two children. Our girls have moved to distant cities. His two boys are still nearby. I could get to Mom's place in less than ten minutes whenever they called to say there was a problem or she was lonesome and wanted me to come.

Mom said to me quite a few months ago: aging is not for the faint of heart. That's what she said when she greeted me one morning when I came to visit her. She smiled when she said it to be sure I understood it was a reality, not a complaint. I learned so much from Mom and the people at the retirement home about what it was like to grow old.

I remembered one day wheeling her into the busy dining room of the retirement home.

Hey Mom. This is a treat. We're going to have lunch together. I'll move your wheelchair just a bit so you're not bumping into the table leg. Are you comfortable? Can you reach your fork and spoon?

She interrupted me, Look there's my neighbor at the next table. She's having trouble sitting down. Her walker's in the way. Please go and help her. She's such a poor old lady. I always look out for her.

Yes, Mom.

That was Mom. She never considered herself to be a poor old lady having so much difficulty. Don't you see yourself? I wanted to shout. How can you ignore your own incapacity and be so compassionate to others?

For the last two years Mom had not been able to stand on her own. She spent the day in a wheelchair. She was blind in one eye and could no longer see well enough to read. She was quite deaf. She had to be hoisted in and out of bed with a mini-crane-like mechanism. She looked terrified when she was hanging there in the supportive sling between her bed and the chair.

She couldn't have her meals in the main dining room anymore because she wasn't able to eat on her own or carry on conversations with her table mates. When I came at lunch or dinnertime I would feed her soft food and hold her cup. She still liked the taste of coffee, but with more cream and sugar than she used to take. The nurses crushed her pills.

I wanted to ask her, With all these frailties to bear, how can you have such a joyful demeanor? How can you be so calm and peaceful? How can you always smile and welcome us when we come to see you?

How can I find your sense of peace? I wondered. I hope I learn your secret one day.

I visited whenever I could, usually three or four times a week. I came when I had a couple of hours between meetings and appointments in my overly scheduled daily agenda. I showed up, sometimes somewhat reluctantly I had to admit, thinking, I know Mom will miss me if I don't come. I really should go and see her. But I came to realize that I was the one who would have missed not being with her.

Some days the time I spent with her was the only quiet time I had when I could collect my thoughts and think about what I was doing.

She always asked, How are you? And what about your husband and your girls? What are they up to? And I knew she was listening to me, hearing me, giving me her full attention. As no one else would do.

Mom and I had two special dates I tried never to miss. Every Sunday we went to the little church two blocks from the retirement home. Afterward we had lunch together. Sometimes when the weather was sunny and warm enough to sit outside we met my husband at the pub farther along the street. There was a ramp up to the wide front porch and I could easily maneuver her into an out-of-the-way corner. Mom and I would share a smoked salmon omelet with fries or pancakes and maple syrup and she would help herself to a few sips of my draft cider.

For the last four or five months we hadn't gone out for lunch. After the first snowfall in November it was too hard for me to push her wheelchair outside, so we watched a church service on TV in the quiet of her room. I brought food to share, mainly homemade soup and pudding, easy for her to swallow. After our lunch I tucked her in for a nap and went home to have lunch again with my husband. My brother usually came by later in the afternoon or early evening to visit with her. That was our Sunday routine.

On Wednesday mornings I joined Mom and some of the residents for a short service in the retirement home chapel led by the plainspoken pastor who arrived faithfully in all kinds of weather. He read a scripture passage and gave us a brief homily to reflect on. It's a practice run for my Sunday program, he would say. What's your favorite hymn? Everyone had a turn to choose. We were a small community. About a dozen regulars, sometimes a few more, sometimes a few less. The faces changed. New arrivals at the retirement home. Departures. Sickness and death.

The retirement home where Mom lived from the age of eighty-five to ninety-four marked every holiday on the calendar with enthusiasm. Families were encouraged to join in and we always did. Valentine's, St. Patrick's, Easter, Mother's Day, Father's Day and the first of July. Then a long summer in between with picnics, barbeques and brass bands playing on the lawn in the back garden, followed by Thanksgiving, Remembrance Day, Christmas and New Year's. The entrance lobby, the hallways and the dining room were decorated festively and there was a special program of activities to make the event memorable. It was the evening dances that were the most fun, especially at New Year's and Valentine's.

Valentine's Day was Mom's favorite festivity. Perhaps because it was the first celebration after the New Year, a party in the middle of cold bleak winter, and it was an event new to her when she came here from Europe. Red and pink, bright colors everywhere, in the stores, in the flower shops, in our home, all those years ago. Mom would always buy a bouquet of red tulips to remind her of Holland where she'd lived during World War Two. She would set out the red heart cards we'd made at school along with the one from Dad—if he remembered—all carefully arranged on the round coffee table by the window.

I recalled one Valentine's three or four years ago. Snow on the ground. Pink and red lights looped around the pillars of the retirement home entrance. Cheerful colors reflected in the icicles hanging from the roof. It was early evening and my husband and two daughters, who were still living at home, dropped me off at the front door and went to park the car. I carried our dessert down the long corridor to Mom's room.

Look Mom. I held the cake out for her to see. Just as you always made it. Heart-shaped, chocolate, white icing, red cinnamon candies for decoration. I have your cake tins now. You gave them to me when you came here. The heart-shaped tins you always kept in the cupboard under the sink of your small apartment. You're the one who baked for every special occasion. Now I'm trying to do that for all our family celebrations.

I went down to the retirement home kitchen for plates, forks, serviettes and cups of coffee. My brother arrived with his wife and two sons.

Great to see you. I rushed over to greet my nephews. Bend down so I can give you big hugs. You're both getting so tall. I don't see much of either of you these days, even though you're just a few streets away. The girls are here too. They're out parking the car.

We crowded into Mom's small room, sitting on the bed, on the floor. The cake on her round coffee table by the window. The bouquet of red tulips set aside to make space for our plates.

Great cake. Just like you always made, Mom.

She smiled and said, Thank you, as if she'd baked it herself.

Hey, are you going dancing? my husband called out. He was always impatient sitting around too long at family gatherings. I can hear the music starting up in the dining room.

The four kids ran ahead. The rest of us behind. Mom in her wheelchair.

Can she hear the music? I wondered. Mom and Dad had loved to dance. What is she thinking? Or is she just happy we're all here together?

An elderly couple was walking ahead of us into the dining room where the musicians were playing a lively song from the big band era, "Fly Me to the Moon," an old favorite of mine.

The old lady was wearing a plain gray pleated skirt and a white blouse with a gold circle brooch on the collar, walking hesitantly, stooping slightly. Her husband was in a suit, loose fitting now, shuffling a bit in his slippers. They stopped and listened. They turned to each other and smiled as if they were remembering some other time. They moved together. All the hesitation disappeared as their feet followed the familiar pattern of the dance steps and they were in that moment when they heard the music so long ago.

I recalled how joyful Mom had been that evening. Talking and laughing. Enjoying our family get-together. We were all there—the nine of us—celebrating together with her.

I remembered another Valentine's Day a year after Dad died seventeen years ago. I was visiting Mom. She was still living on her own in the apartment she and Dad had moved into after they sold our family home.

What day is it tomorrow? she asked.

Valentine's, Mom.

Your father always sent me a Valentine in the mail, she said. Once a really big one. I had to fold it in half to save it in my dresser drawer. He wasn't very good at expressing his thoughts but he tried to in the Valentine cards.

Do you remember? she continued. They found him dead in the parking lot of the shopping center. Heart attack, they said. They said it was a good thing he hadn't turned the car on and driven away. He had a bag beside him on the seat—apples and prunes—what he was supposed to get.

The police came to the door, she recalled. They told me what had happened. I went to the hospital. They showed him to me. His eyes were still open. I looked into them. I looked down, down into endless emptiness. I closed them. He was gone. They asked a nurse to stay with me for a while in case I got hysterical, I suppose. There I was, in a moment—a widow. No longer a wife. It was so unexpected. I never thought it would happen.

Do you remember? They laid out your father in his navy blazer with his medals from World War Two pinned on the breast pocket. Some ladies asked me if he had a Cross for Valor. I said no, but he should have. He was so brave. He always looked after his men. So many died, he sometimes told me. So many young men. They were not prepared.

Mom continued with her memories. I asked my brothers, she said, why are you going to war? All three of them. Dead. They were so sure they would come back. I think of all the cemeteries, all those white crosses. Every one marks a life.

That was the day before Valentine's, the year after Dad died. There we were, Mom, you and I. Mourning Dad. Your brothers. A long time ago.

I opened my eyes. I must have dozed a bit in the chair beside Mom's bed. She was still quietly sleeping. I looked around her room. There was the tulip plant I'd bought this morning at the gift shop on the main floor. Perhaps that was what brought all those Valentine's memories to mind.

And here I am today, Mom, I wanted to say to her. You and I in your hospital room. What will Valentine's be like without you? And what about all my memories of our times together these last nine years at the retirement home? No more Sunday lunches. No more Wednesday services. How can that be? Who will I share them with now? What will death be like? How can I bear this, Mom?

All my unanswered questions. No answers.

I am afraid.
You're dying.
Your death.
What will it be like?
When will I understand?
Where will I find
your sense of peace?

I am so afraid.

Still day six. Late afternoon. I was sitting beside Mom's hospital bed. Remembering. Endless memories chaotically flooding through my mind. I was getting tired. But I didn't want to leave in case she woke up.

3

Mom and I were very close. We'd shared so much. As a six-year-old, I cried with her when she got the terrible news her father had died and then, a year later, her mother. As a teenager, I supported her through the depression and mania of bipolar disease and the long recovery from cancer. Dad was there too, of course, but he didn't seem very good at comforting Mom. As a mother with a family of my own, I looked after her when Dad died and she fell back into depression. I cared for her all the time right up until now.

Mother. Daughter. Caregiver. Our roles had always been intertwined.

In more recent years, since Mom had moved to the retirement home, she sometimes called me her "Mom." I remembered how that could cause quite a scene at the retirement home. One day I was late for my regular Wednesday morning visit, and there was a new caregiver.

Mom asks her, Where's my Mom? She's late. She's never late.

The caregiver doesn't quite know how to respond but, very gently and kindly, she says, I think perhaps you are mistaken.

Your mother passed on long ago.

No. No, that cannot be. Mom begins to cry inconsolably.

I arrive just at that moment. She smiles at me and all is well again.

I explain to the caregiver who is now very upset, Mom sometimes calls me Mom. It's okay now.

I had been Mom's caregiver, Mom's Mom, for a long time. She had been sick a lot in her life, physically and mentally, and she had to bear an enormous burden of loss. Too much sadness.

Sitting there in Mom's hospital room, I remembered being six years old, more than fifty years ago. I come home from school, running through the house looking for her. Calling out, Mom, where are you? She is always in the kitchen waiting for me. I find her upstairs, sitting on the edge of her bed, crying and crying. Mom. Mom. What's wrong?

I'm frightened. I've never seen Mom cry before. I don't know what to do. She holds out a black-edged card. Her hands are shaking. I can't read the words. The letters are heavy in a strange-looking script. I don't understand.

My father died, she says. I was not there to receive his blessing, to say goodbye. I was not there to comfort my mother. How can this be?

I sit down on the floor beside her and cry with her not understanding why until Dad comes home.

As soon as Mom could make the arrangements to travel to Europe, she went to visit her mother in the home she had grown up in. She took me and my brother with her. I had just turned seven.

We stayed with my Oma from July to October 1956. I went to school there for three months. Every day Oma and Mom talked and talked. Sometimes they cried too. I didn't always understand what they were saying. When Mom tucked me into bed at night in the little room up in the attic, which had once been hers, I would ask, What were you and Oma talking about? Why were you crying? And Mom would tell me. Most of her stories were sad. So many deaths. I didn't always understand. We would lie there together on my bed crying.

Mom told me her three brothers were killed in World War Two. I had seen their photos hanging in a row over Mom's bed at home. And one of her father and mother. Beside the photos was a cherry wood cross.

I knew about the cherry tree. Mom had told me the cherry wood came from one of the trees in the big garden behind her parent's house. She showed me where it had grown. Her father, my Opa, had cut it down years ago because it was dead. He had made the photograph frames and the cross from the wood. She showed me the young cherry tree that grew beside the old one. It was beautiful, full of fruit the summer I was there with Mom visiting my Oma. I climbed the ladder, which was propped against it, and ate the cherries right there up in the tree. I had never done that before.

Mom told me stories about her brothers. Her favorite, a year older than she was, with bright auburn hair just like hers, had been a fighter pilot. He was shot down at sea. His body never found. No grave. No marker. Her youngest brother, nine years younger, the baby brother she had so hoped would be a sister, had been a foot soldier. He had died of terrible battle wounds. She once showed me the letter her parents received from the chaplain at the field hospital. So young, he wrote, your son's last words: Tell my parents and my dear sister I love you so much. Her oldest brother, perhaps most tragically of all, was killed two months after he was discharged with highest honors from active service. He was shot down on a mountain road as he was moving his wife and young son to a safer place. His son, Mom's only nephew, her parent's first grandchild, died soon after his father of a head injury incurred when he fell down as he and his mother were fleeing enemy fire. His wife, Mom's sister-in-law, survived the war, remarried and moved to South America. She was a beautiful woman. I have seen her photo but we never met. She cut off all contact with her husband's family after the war. Perhaps she just wanted to forget everything that had happened.

Before the war Mom had married a Dutchman and moved from Germany, where she was born, to Holland. Her first husband was killed too. All those family members I never knew. Then Mom met Dad in Holland. He was part of the Canadian Forces that liberated the country at the end of the war. They married and Mom came over as a war bride to start a new life here.

Mom's parents came from Europe once to visit us and stayed from Mother's Day until mid-November 1954. I had just turned five. I remembered the evening they arrived.

Mom and Dad received a phone call that morning to say her parents had disembarked their ship in the port of Montreal and were traveling by train to our home town. My parents drove to the station to greet them. A friend came over to babysit my brother and me. I was so excited. It was way past my bedtime and no one seemed to notice. I was sitting in my pajamas half asleep on the top stairs. Suddenly the front door opened and they stepped into the light of the hallway.

Opa was wearing a black suit with a wing collared white shirt and dark tie. He had a huge white beard. Oma was in a black coat and wide black hat and gloves. I came down the stairs a bit tentatively. I was not usually shy, but they seemed very old and strangely dressed. They were smiling and talking to me, but I couldn't understand what they were saying. Oma reached down to kiss me and started to cry. Why was that? Opa picked me up. He hugged me and his beard tickled my cheek. I giggled as I pulled away rubbing my face. The grown-ups laughed at my surprise. I was sent off to bed. That was all I remembered from our first meeting.

Our languages separated us, but we hugged and laughed as they watched us play. They were so happy to see us—my younger brother and me—their only grandchildren. That one visit, those six short months. The next year my Opa died and then my Oma, a year later.

Mom was very sad for a long time after that. I tried to comfort her and make her feel happy that she still had us—Dad, my brother and me.

Whenever we were alone together, Mom would tell me her stories. Most of them were about the war and her brothers and sometimes about her family when she was growing up. She rarely spoke of her early experiences of being here, of arriving as a war bride in a strange country. Or maybe I forgot. But there was one story that stayed with me. The story of losing her first child, the older brother I always wished I had. She was pregnant on the ship coming over from Holland in November 1946. The seas were rough, she told me, and she got seasick. She was anxious about what her new life would be like. She had never met any of Dad's family or his friends except his wartime buddies.

She had always lived in the city, never in a small town in a rural area. It was an enormous transition for her. Dad had registered for a wartime house, one of thirty thousand the government had built in many communities after the war to provide affordable housing for returning veterans and their families. When Mom arrived in our small town, she and Dad lived with his oldest sister until their child was to be born and they could move into the new house assigned to them. But when the baby was stillborn the allocation was rescinded.

I had written a poem about how I thought she must have felt after she lost her baby and she and Dad had to stay on at his sister's house. The words were simple, easily memorized. I whispered them to her as I sat there beside her. Mom silent in her hospital bed, me lost in endless memories.

Cabin fever.
You told me
how it felt
sitting alone
reading
in the room
shared
with your husband
in the house
shared
with your sister-in-law.
No where else to live.
Not now.

You lost your first-born son.
Your name stroked off the list.
Wartime houses were for
veterans with families.
No family.
No house.

You told me
about cabin fever.
How you read the early pioneers
suffered through long winters,
closeted in log cabins. Distant
from friends and loved ones.
Sitting alone reading
in their one-room house.

I saw you
sitting alone
reading
in your wheelchair
in your room
in the retirement home.
Cabin fever?

Sometimes Mom repeated her stories over and over, especially the sad ones about the deaths of her brothers and her own wartime experiences. But she never spoke about what she suffered. I wished now that I had insisted she tell me how she coped with all that sorrow, what it was like to bear so much sadness. It might have helped me now.

Perhaps telling the stories was her way of coping. Perhaps that was how she lived with all the deaths of her loved ones and the loneliness of leaving her home country and coming here to a strange land. I don't think she ever got over her deep sadness. She just soldiered on. As the years passed and she became ill with bipolar disease and cancer, she became more fragile.

When I was eleven Mom told me her doctor said she had breast cancer. I remembered thinking, now I have to do everything my mother does. I have to make the meals for my father and my brother, and I have to keep the house tidy. She might die. Mom might die. I was scared. But I also felt strangely grown-up. I would have to look after everyone now.

Afterward Mom showed me the scar. Through all my teenage years I was afraid I would have to have my breast removed too.

Genetic, maybe, the doctor said, but he wasn't sure. Two years later the same doctor told Mom she had cancer of the bladder. Again she went for surgery and chemotherapy. She survived that too.

Close to my sixteenth birthday, Mom was diagnosed with bipolar disease, manic depression they called it then. At first Dad wouldn't let me go to visit her in the psychiatric hospital —the loony bin as the kids at school called it, teasing me.

But I insisted. Dad, I've sat by her bed for hours sometimes when you are at work. She cries and cries. She won't get up. I can't get her dressed. She won't eat. I know how she is. I must see her.

Dad agreed to take me after school on my birthday. He said, Your Mom has something for you. I remembered being kind of excited. I liked surprises.

It's getting dark. The psychiatric hospital looks scary, like a medieval fortress. Our feet crunch on the gravel walkway to the entrance of ward one, the admittance ward. The door is heavy with grates over the glass. We push the buzzer. We step inside. I feel the air hot and dry rush outside behind me. The door slams shut. There's a strange acrid smell. I can't describe it, disinfectants maybe, but I recognize it again here in this hospital. I hear low moaning and a sharp cry. I can't look. I don't want to see. Dad leads me to Mom's room. She's sitting very still in a large chair. She's wearing a strange blue-flowered gown. She looks crushed.

Dad, I whisper, why is Mom wearing that dress. You know she hates blue. She says it doesn't suit her auburn hair. Even though the bright red had long ago faded to dark brunette.

I rush over to hug her. She smiles a bit. She has a royal blue sweater on her lap. She holds it up. For me. For my birthday. I know how much she loves to knit. It calms me, she always says. She must have made this for me while she was here in the hospital from the wool we bought together months ago. I had forgotten all about it. Blue is my favorite color.

I held onto that sweater for a long time. I kept it in a drawer full of memory things. I liked the way it smelled and felt. Warm and musty and familiar.

Mom eventually came back home. At first she seemed better but she wasn't healed. One morning a few months later, when I was helping her get ready for another visit to the psychiatric hospital, I remembered pleading with her, Please Mom, get up. Let me help you get dressed. Please eat some breakfast. I have to go to school, Mom. Dad's already at work but he'll be back soon. I can't leave you like this. Crying. Please Mom.

Mom's suitcase lay open on her bedroom floor. Empty. She was still in bed crying.

Dad says we have to pack, I tell her. You have an appointment with the psychiatrist. What are you taking?

Nothing, she whispers.

What? That's crazy. I walk over to her dressing table. I see us reflected in the mirror. I'm sixteen. Tall. Blond. Looking cross.

It's my birthday next week. My sixteenth. Sweet sixteen. Oh yeah, sure. Mom's going to the hospital again for treatment. They won't even tell me for how long. Who's going to bake my cake? Mom's still crying. Will she ever get over this? I pick up her hairbrush, her green velvet vanity case, terra-cotta-colored lipstick, brown eyebrow pencil, face powder.

Dad comes in. She doesn't need any clothes, he says. They'll give her something to wear.

That's weird, I think, having to wear the hospital's clothes.

How about shoes?

No.

Slippers?

Yes.

I pick up her favorite ones—ivory satin mules. She used to let me clomp around in them when I was a kid.

No the others.

Are you sure? They're so ugly. Those elastic-sided, fold-up ones old women carry around in their handbags. Something to put on when they take off their winter boots at church hall meetings. Are you sure that's all she needs? I close up the almost empty suitcase.

Dad helps Mom down the stairs and they go out to the car. I sit on the steps and cry. In anger and frustration. Helpless to help Mom.

Mom returned to the psychiatric hospital on a number of occasions. She was given shock treatments. I once asked her, What is that like?

She said, There is a moment when I cannot breathe. I am sure I will die and then I black out. That's how I experience it anyway. Maybe it's different for others.

Mom remained in a stable mental condition for about four years. She took up weaving again. She bought a small table-sized loom. During the war she had operated a large commercial loom in Holland, designing and skillfully weaving beautiful tapestries, including an award-winning piece that had been submitted to the 1934 Chicago World's Fair. At home she worked on a smaller scale, but she nevertheless joyfully rediscovered her creativity after so many years being Mom and homemaker and battling so much sickness. Friends in our township raised sheep, goats and llamas for wool, so she introduced natural colors, textures, handmade dyes and new patterns into her weaving.

She also graduated with the first class of Registered Nursing Assistants at our local hospital, coming as near as she could to fulfilling her life-long dream to be a nurse, a dream she had to give up as a young woman when it was discovered she had a heart murmur.

I was still in high school and living at home. I worked at our local psychiatric hospital for two summers as a nurses' aide. Why did I do that? Why did I put myself back into the very ward where I had once visited Mom? I wondered. All these years later

I still think it was a very strange thing to do. Was I curious to know how others experienced mental illness? How they were treated? Did they recover and go home? Had the caregiver role already become so ingrained in me that I felt I needed to be constantly helping others? A simpler answer was that the pay was good for a summer job and I was saving to attend university with plans to go into psychiatry, a plan I abandoned after two years in the program. When Mom's bipolar symptoms returned I realized I could not face working in an environment where I had spent so many troubling times visiting her.

During my first summer working at the hospital I befriended a young woman about my age who was diagnosed with schizophrenia. I liked her. I brought her trendy scarves and belts I thought would suit her. I visited her during my lunch break whenever I could. One day we were chatting in her room and she called me over to the window to look out at something. As I leaned forward to see she grabbed a coat hanger she had laid on the wide stone sill and tried to wrap it around my neck. I was taller and stronger and really had no trouble fighting her off.

I was shocked. I didn't understand. I thought she liked me. My supervisor switched me to a different ward. A few days later I heard she had broken a glass and tried to swallow the pieces. I couldn't believe she could do that to herself.

Two years later, after I left home for university in a nearby city, Mom had a relapse and was sent to a private psychiatric clinic located in the same city. While she was there I went to visit her every day after classes.

Where are you going? my house mates would ask. Off to the library again? You are the studious one aren't you?

How could I tell them my mother was in a mental institution just down the street from where we lived? I went to see her in the clinic on my twenty-first birthday—April 30—just as I had visited her in the psychiatric ward on my sixteenth. She had knitted me a beret and matching scarf in forest green mohair wool. Her favorite color, not mine. Unworn. Stored in the same drawer at home with my well-worn blue sweater.

Dad and I wrote each other long letters during my four years at university. Cheaper than long distance charges. A few months ago I found a bundle of letters from him.

In one he wrote, Life has been very difficult for your mother these last few weeks. She misses you a lot and always counts on you to be there for her. As you know yourself, only too well, her times of depression are very hard on her. I'm always surprised that she pulls herself out of the depressed moods she slips into periodically and with psychiatric help bounces back to normal for a period. We are all so happy thinking finally this is it. But then the depression or the mania returns and we go through the whole unpleasant routine again. But at least she is able to come back each time, and that is something to be grateful for.

That was the hardest time of my life to care for Mom. I was away from home trying to make friends and get on at university. I felt I couldn't tell anyone about Mom's mental illness. I thought she was weak and vulnerable and she was making my life very difficult. I was ashamed of her. I was angry too that she wasn't there to help me get settled. I didn't understand then how strong she really was and how resilient. She somehow managed to cope with the sadness and loneliness of the deaths she had to bear and the illnesses she had to suffer. She survived all those traumas. She became a loving grandmother to our two girls and my brother's two boys. And she lived to be ninety-four.

I didn't learn any coping skills from her. I had to take on the role of mother/caregiver without knowing how to deal with her losses or mine either—not having the mother I would have liked to have had to help me sort through the challenges of young adulthood.

Looking back, I often wondered, when did Mom begin to recover from the bipolar disorder? Did she ever really heal completely? Did she continue to have bouts of mania and depression long after that I didn't know about? Chose not to remember? I recall once my father yelling at her. She'd bought a cherry wood china cabinet during one manic phase and an expensive outfit—a lovely silk dress and matching coat in rich green and brown tones which suited her very well. Dad felt we couldn't afford them. He wanted her to take them back. But they were both fine purchases. She had very good taste.

Mom was eventually prescribed lithium pills which stabilized her for long periods of time. But she continued to struggle with violent mood swings. She spent time in our local psychiatric hospital to have her drugs monitored or changed, and after Dad died she continued to suffer severe bouts of loneliness.

That was seventeen years ago. My brother and I helped Mom move to a small apartment not far from the house we grew up in so she could stay in touch with her friends and neighbors and the church we had always attended together. For a while we continued to go to that church whenever we came to visit Mom and I took her to the ladies' missionary society group, especially on her birthday when they organized a spring tea. I visited every week. It was about an hour's drive from where we live now. We had fun together shopping for clothes, buying groceries—the heavier things she could not carry home from her local corner store, lunch in our favorite cafe. But then we moved Mom to a retirement home closer to where we live. More convenient for us, but distant from her friends.

One day three years after Dad's passing, I phoned and her voice sounded strange, sort of slurred and muffled. I drove as fast as I could to her apartment. I found her lying on the bedroom floor beside the phone. I pulled her up onto the bed and tried to make her sit. But she was like a rag doll. She was barely able to stand. Somehow, half dragging, half carrying, I got her into my car. We sat for hours in the emergency waiting room. She slumped down more and more in her chair. She seemed to be slipping away. Finally she got a bed and the doctors began to assess what was wrong. Her kidneys were shutting down. Lithium toxicity. She hadn't been monitoring her intake of the drug, the drug that had seemed such a miracle solution to stabilize her moods. Dad had been the one to remind her. Now it would be up to me.

I sat up abruptly. Too many memories for one day. Turbulent, unsettling. I pulled myself back to the present. Here I was still sitting beside Mom's bed waiting for her to wake up. I was exhausted after the trip home from my holidays and receiving the terrible news she might not make it through the night, my awful guilt that I wasn't there when she needed me, and my long watch until dawn. I had looked after Mom for so many years. I knew she had been waiting for me. The nurse said so. Why hadn't I come when I first heard the news? Had she given up because I wasn't there? I didn't know. She wasn't responding to me at all.

4

Day seven. Noon. Saturday. I was back at the hospital to continue my vigil. Seven days since Mom was rushed to emergency. Two days since I returned from my holiday. One day after the start of spring, March 21—just yesterday. I missed celebrating St. Patrick's Day with Mom. Why? Because I was away. I would never forgive myself for not coming back the moment I heard she was ill.

St. Patrick's was another of Mom's favorite spring celebrations—after Valentine's. Strange really because March 17 was the birthday of her first baby who was stillborn. But then she celebrated the birthdays of all her long dead brothers and her parents. She never made it a sad thing. She just wanted to remember them she said. Remember to remember. And we loved the specially decorated green-iced, home-baked cakes she made for us.

Mom liked the color green and wore it frequently so of course she would wear something green on St. Pat's. She would try to make me do the same, but I always resisted except for a small green bow pinned to my collar. Not my color. She loved spring flowers and plants. Red tulips for Valentine's. Bright green shamrocks in a pot. I had bought Mom some more red tulips that morning at the florist shop downstairs in the hospital mall. They were still in bud so they should last awhile.

5

Day eight. Sunday. I brought my journal with me to the hospital. The one I began at Christmas. Three months ago. I intended to read Mom some of her stories that I'd written down. The ones she had once told me. I hoped desperately that hearing my voice would wake her up. I guessed she was in a coma, but no one on the medical team explained to me why that was or when or if she was going to wake up. Maybe they didn't know either.

I opened my journal. The first entry. I began to read out loud. I changed some of the words to make it sound as if I was speaking to Mom.

We're all together, still sitting at the dining table after our Christmas Eve meal, my husband and our two girls, my brother and his wife, their two sons and you, Mom. The nine of us, our little family after Dad died. I've pulled your wheelchair up close to the table so I can hold your cup and feed you some pudding. We're looking at photos. Here's one I know will make you smile. It's from Christmas a few years ago. You're wearing a funny green reindeer headband with bright red antlers. Do you remember? I can see you smiling.

You haven't said anything all evening, but I'm sure you're enjoying being here with us. You look up from the photo and you begin to hum an old familiar melody and then you sing softly but quite distinctly in German, words you've said to me so many times before: "This moment together can only happen once. This moment together will never come again. It is too wonderful to be real. Life can only bring us here this once, just as every spring has only one May."

I stopped reading. I couldn't go on. That memory was too intense. It was making me cry. And anyway I didn't think she was hearing me. I sat there for a while my journal open on my lap.

When I started my journal several months ago my plan was to record everything Mom said. In the weeks after Christmas and into the New Year, she'd gradually lost the ability to speak altogether. Or maybe she just didn't want to speak anymore. Everything she said suddenly seemed important to remember. She was speaking fewer and fewer words.

I didn't realize then how important my journaling would be. That writing down my memories of the times we had shared would help me prepare for losing her and, ultimately, for working my way through my grieving.

I continued reading to myself.

Just after Christmas I had written: Our conversations would have been amusing to anyone listening in. I would carry on both sides of our conversation, hers and mine.

We're having our coffee at the round table beside the window in Mom's familiar retirement home room. I wrap her hands around her mug and put my own over top and together we raise the mug to her lips. She takes a few small sips.

I ask her a question. Something simple. How are you doing today, Mom?

She smiles and looks at me. But no response. I answer for her, Quite well.

Yes, you are looking really well. It's a lovely day outside. Almost Valentine's. They're putting up the red balloons and the pink and red hearts. You always enjoy that special celebration. Remember?

Nod. Smile. And so we continue our one-sided conversation.

I tell her I've been invited to sit on the board of our local art gallery, that our girls are doing well at university. I tell her my husband is traveling quite a bit for work and that he hates being away from home. I tell her my brother will be in to visit tomorrow evening. I tell her about some world events.

Mid-February, I described an e-mail from our older daughter telling her Oma how much fun she had skiing. I read it to Mom. And Mom actually spoke a sentence. She said, My dearest oldest granddaughter, she has lots of opportunities to have fun where she's living now, but too far away.

A few pages further on in my journal, I wrote that our younger daughter, who is an artist and musician, sent the photo her friend had taken during his Christmas visit, a photo of our hands intertwined: mine, Mom's and my younger daughter's. She'd stayed on with us for a few more days after her sister returned to her own place on the West Coast. I showed it to Mom and she spoke another sentence. She said, This is so lovely. Our hands, our three generations intertwined. Put it there on my bookshelf so I can see it.

Full comprehensive sentences. Then there were days with no words at all. I noted that it seemed to be tangibles—the e-mail, the photo that stimulated Mom's responses. So I looked around her room for something that would prompt a story. I saw the photo that had been on her chest of drawers for as long as I could remember—my parents' wedding photo. Mom and Dad face to face. Surprise, delight in their eyes. The tall, slim, sandy haired young man, handsome in his Cameron Highlanders uniform and the new bride in her form-fitting long-sleeved brown velvet wedding dress.

I picked up the photo and held it out to her. Remember this day? Remember the story you always told me about how you met Dad? She smiled. No response. So I began to tell her that story. Her story, in her voice, the way she had always told it to me.

Mom's Story: Meeting Dad

It's June 1945. I watched the soldiers march into Soest, the small town just outside The Hague where I lived through the war.

The Canadian Forces have liberated Holland!
The Canadians are here.
Cheering crowds out in the streets.
Everyone is celebrating.

I was there in the jubilant crowds that lined the streets waving and cheering as the tanks and troop carriers passed by. I was in my best and only suit, made of men's worsted wool fabric, which was all I could get from the black market. Dark brown with a thin pale gray stripe running through it, chocolate brown wool sweater, and my hair—it was still bright auburn then—pinned up under my felt hat.

Cheering crowds out in the streets.
Everyone is celebrating.

Your Dad was there marching down the street, a Cameron Highlander, part of the Canadian Liberation Forces. He had found lodgings for each of his men with local families happy to share their homes for a few nights with the Canadian soldiers who had brought a victorious end to the war. He needed a place to stay for himself. He asked a young woman standing at the corner if she knew anyone who would billet a soldier for a few days until temporary barracks were constructed.

Yes, she'd replied. My next-door neighbor has a whole house to herself. Her husband died in the war and she lives alone now. Perhaps she will rent you a room for a few days.

I return home after the parade relieved it's finally over. This terrible war that has killed my three brothers.

I hear the crunch of a man's footsteps on my walkway. A knock on my front door. For a fleeting moment I think, could it be my brother? I've been thinking of him all day. Has he finally come home? No. That cannot be. He's dead.

I open the door. I'm still dressed in my best suit. The one with the narrow fitted waist and pencil slim skirt. He looks surprised. What does he expect, a *hausfrau* in her apron?

He introduces himself.
Explains why he's there.
I nod.
Smile slightly.
He reaches out his hand.
I invite him inside.
That's how we met, your Dad and I.

When I finished telling the story, I'd asked Mom, Did I get it right? Are there any details I should add? No response. I was too late. There would be no new stories now. I would have to draw on my own memories.

That day in late February I went home and wrote down her story in my journal, just as I had told it to her, her story about meeting Dad. A few days later when I visited I read it back to her. I remembered how delighted she'd been. She nodded full of smiles and clapped her hands. Yes. Yes, that is just the way it was. Hearing her own story seemed to make her happy. Her favorite story.

I started to tell her other stories she had once told me: about her childhood, the only girl with three teasing brothers, her life in Holland during the war, meeting Dad, immigrating to Canada and starting a new life here. I tried to remember all the stories she had ever told me. I asked my brother too. I wrote them all down in my journal.

Mom's Story: Trading Black Market Soap and Chocolate for Food

I enjoy riding my bicycle through the quaint villages and forested parklands here in Holland where I'm living now. It's so flat beside the seashore dunes. But now it's the dead of night. I'm on a lonely country road. Out of town. Way past curfew. No one is allowed to move about at night. It's wartime November 1943. I had to take this risk because I must get food for myself and the old man and his wife who are living in my house.

They are from the south of Holland. Farmers. The dykes were bombed last week and all the fields flooded. They made it to high ground but with nothing. The civilian government installed by the Nazis in my city—The Hague—ordered us to billet them and all the others. No food. They sit huddled by my fire every day. All day long. I never use the fireplace myself. Firewood is precious, but they're in shock I guess. The man especially hardly says a word. They have a cousin who has a farm not too far from the city. We manage to make contact and arrange for me to go there to buy food from him. He will trade some potatoes and turnips and, maybe, a piece of meat for the soap and chocolate I have managed to get on the black market.

I made it safely to the farm. Got the food even some meat. His wife was glad to have the soap and chocolate. Now I'm so exhausted. I begged the cousin to let me stay the night and go back the next day but he refused.

He said, What if they come and find you here? You're out after curfew. I'll be in trouble.

Let me stay a few hours at least.

I lay down in my coat by the fire. He woke me up. You must go now. It was so dark and cold. My bicycle is very heavy with the bags of potatoes and turnips. I can barely see the narrow dirt road. I keep veering off into the ditches. But I'm getting closer to the city. Home. I have to get there before daylight so no one will see me. I get off the road now and take a shortcut across the fields to avoid being surprised by any military vehicles. I can just see the crumbling stone wall in front of me. It was a barn before it fell down. I remember it from last night. Around that wall and I will be able to see the first houses at the edge of town. It will be easier on the pavement.

Halt! Soldiers leaning against the wall smoking. They look so relaxed. Boys really. Remind me of my brothers. One walks toward me.

He shouts, What are you doing? What have you got there?

I'm stunned. They will take everything. They will arrest me. Curfew. No, I shout back.

For a moment, they are my three brothers. They are teasing me. Trying to steal my dolls. Trying to take the chocolate I kept to eat slowly when they ate theirs all at one go. I will not let them have it. I can hold my own. I always do.

No. You will not have it. It's mine!

The soldier walking toward me stops. Surprised. A Dutch woman speaking German. He grabs my arm roughly. What are you doing here? What have you got in those bags?

I'm still shouting, No. No. I burst into hysterical tears.

They're all gathered around me now. Boys. Curious. Something interesting. What is this? What's happening?

I tell them everything. I am German born. I married a Dutchman. He was killed in the war. I live here now in The Hague. I have two old people billeted in my house and they need food. I had to go out into the country at night to get to the farm. I wait. What will they do?

Their leader decides. They will take everything. All my bags. Tonight they will drop them over the low stone wall at the front of my house.

I caution them. Do not let anyone see you. My neighbors are already suspicious of me because they know I can speak German.

They tell me, Go now. Quickly. And be sure not to get caught.

Why were Mom's stories so important to me, especially at the end of her life? They let me picture her as a spirited, independent, attractive young woman. They erased for a moment the present image of an old lady, infirm, in her wheelchair, dying in a hospital bed. When I read her these stories we banished death for a little while. I also believed I had to record them because they gave value to her life and created a sense of continuum from generation to generation. Her father understood the importance of doing that. Mom had given me the book in which he had painstakingly traced his family, relative by relative, back to 1758. I appreciated that sense of being part of something bigger—a chain of lives linked backward and forward. I was a link in that chain and I wanted to build on that continuity, keep it going. I wanted to be sure Mom was not forgotten, and in my own selfish way I knew that if I wrote about her I would not be forgotten.

I thought to myself, Perhaps this is what we must do to bear our own mortality, our ultimate death, to know that there is an ongoing story of which we are a part. I read her those stories over and over again, and others I wrote down. We laughed as we shared her memories. We sat by the window in her room with our cups of coffee from the retirement home dining room. Several flowering plants stood on the small round table. The air was very dry and I was in charge of keeping those plants watered. Mom had a green thumb.

I definitely did not. My husband always teased me that mine was black.

He would say, Any plant you get is likely to die sooner rather than later.

I hated it when he said that but he was right. Even when I did my best to water my plants regularly and keep them in the right light, most didn't survive long.

Mom would always ask me before I went home, Did you remember to water my plants?

Remembering. There I was still sitting by Mom's bed, remembering. I closed the journal I had brought that morning to her hospital room. The bright red tulip plant from the hospital gift shop was on her bedside table. I had remembered to water it, but it appeared small and out of place in the bare beige space. The window looked out at the wall of the next building. Was there enough light? The round black-edged clock was ticking. I was sitting in the same uncomfortable gray leatherette armchair the nurse had pulled up to Mom's bed the first night I had come three days ago. I should bring in Mom's bright yellow wool shawl, I thought. She likes to put it over her shoulders even when it's not so cold.

I opened my journal again and began once more to read Mom's favorite story about meeting Dad. I kept hoping she would finally wake up and smile at me sitting there by her bed reading her story.

But I felt self-conscious hearing my voice out loud. It was so quiet. Was I disturbing anyone? Was she listening? Would someone come in and say, What are you doing? She can't hear you anyway.

I was doubting it too.

I stopped reading. I just sat there, holding her hand, watching her breathe.

I reflected, If anyone had walked in just then, if anyone had seen her lying there, not moving, not speaking, barely even breathing, that person probably would have said, She's an old woman, fragile and vulnerable. She's likely to die soon.

But I just never saw that. I did not want to. I never for a moment considered the possibility of death. I thought, I have to do everything I can to help her get better. What can I do? Who will help? She's safe here in the hospital, in this familiar place where she has been so many times before, where our kids were born, where each of us has been admitted to emergency at one time or another.

I went back to reading to myself all the entries in my journal. I could see how frail she was becoming. I wrote, Just before Valentine's Day. Coughing heavily. When I reach down to hug her good-bye, she says, Can we go home now? What can I say? You are home, Mom. This is your home here in the retirement home.

I continued in my journal, Valentine's Day is surprisingly warm. I help Mom with her coat and hat and put my hand over hers to guide each finger into her gloves. We go outside for a few minutes. I push her along the driveway where the snow has melted back from the foundation walls to reveal tulips in leaf, no blooms yet. Spring won't be long now, Mom.

The week before I left to go away on holidays, I wrote on March 8, Mom seems much worse today. Not wearing her dentures. Having trouble swallowing. There it was, the entry in my journal. I had known she was not well. I had written it down. And still I had left her. Gone on my holidays.

March 13. Visiting Mom to say good-bye. Holding her hands, I'll be back soon. I turn to wave as I leave her sitting there alone in her wheelchair, by the window, beside her small round coffee table.

6

Day nine. I continued to sit by Mom's hospital bed hour after
hour. I frequently lost track of time. I didn't want to leave her. I
was afraid she might wake up and not find me there beside her.

I asked myself, How many days have we been here, Mom, you
and I? You've been here nine days. I've been here only four. They
seem to leave us alone most of the time. What are they waiting
for? The nurses come in and change your IV bag, your life line,
your only form of nourishment. The doctors come in to have a
look at you, but they don't give me a direct answer when I ask
how you're doing. Are you getting better? Are you dying?

We lived in a cocoon those days in the hospital—warm and dry
and disconnected from the rest of life—my life, Mom's life.
Mom and I were there together every day. I had my daily
routine. I came in the morning. I brought my lunch. My
brother sometimes came to spell me off in the afternoon. I
came back in the evening. I was looking after Mom just as I
always did. I called the nurse if any of the monitoring machines
beeped an alarm. I learned how to swab out her mouth with
cold water—just a few drops—using one of those bright pink
sponges on a stick that looked like tiny candy lollipops at a

distance. She seemed safe in that stable, controlled, predictable environment. It gave me time to remember, to slowly come to terms with the transition we were going through, even though I was refusing to accept the truth, that she was unlikely to get better. That she was dying. At that time, I couldn't have admitted it to anyone, including myself.

Late in the afternoon I heard the big stainless steel meal trolley clanking down the hall toward Mom's room. A kitchen staff member brought in her dinner. Gray-green mushy vegetables, a scoop of mashed potato, recognizable, red, brown pureed meat—chicken, beef, veal. It was hard to tell except for the paper menu on the tray. Items checked off— coffee with milk and sugar. She couldn't drink anything. Potatoes, peas, beef, so that was what it was. But she couldn't swallow anything. When I had tried to feed her a few days ago, they said, Don't do that. She might choke.

But how can I sit here and let her starve? I thought suddenly feeling panicky. Maybe I should eat her meal myself so they won't know. It looked unappetizing. Soft in my mouth, tasteless, just salty. She wouldn't have liked it anyway, I thought, except for the coffee.

Suddenly Mom became very agitated as I sat there by her bed. I reached out to hold her hands.   She pushed them away with surprising force. In a frantic voice she said, Do not do anything more for me. Nothing. No thing. Do not help me anymore.

Her first intelligible words since coming here.

What do you mean, Mom? What do you mean by that?

She closed her eyes again. No answer.

I tried to soothe her. Yes, Mom. Yes, I understand.

I understood her words but I did not want to hear what she was saying to me. I did not want to accept what she was trying to tell me.

After a while she grew quite calm. She opened her eyes and said, clearly and distinctly, Thank you for all your loving care. Now I want to go home.

Yes, I said. Yes. Is this her final blessing? I wondered. Is this her good-bye? No. It can't be. Not yet.

Only a few days before I left on holiday, two weeks ago, she had said, I want to go home. I hadn't been sure where she wanted to go, but I was sure she didn't mean her spiritual home.

But what did I know? Where is home?

Mom had finally spoken. The first time after all those days sitting by her bed waiting. I wanted her to say more but that was it. No more words.

7

Day ten. Early morning. I brought a styrofoam cup of coffee from the cafeteria. I was settling into my usual place beside Mom's bed, looking through my journal, wondering if I should try reading Mom one of her stories again in the hope she might respond.

The young doctor hurried in. He spoke to me, direct and business-like, The antibiotics that we have been administering intravenously for the last ten days are going to be withdrawn this morning. The antibiotic cycle is complete. There's nothing more we can do for your mother.

Why is that? I asked quickly, before he turned to stride back out the door. Is she better? Is that why? Is she going to get better? Or do you think she won't get better? Did she respond to the antibiotics? Does she still have pneumonia?

Why won't you tell me? I persisted. I need to know Mom's condition. Why won't anyone answer my questions? Don't you know? Do you know and you don't want to tell me?

Then the social worker came in—out of the blue. In her usual brisk way, she told me, We're discharging your mother at noon today. There's nothing more we can do for her here.

What do you mean? Noon. Today. I was taken completely by surprise. I had no warning. I said, I've only just been told the antibiotic cycle has been completed. I didn't know anything about that.

Yes, the ten-day antibiotic cycle is complete, she replied. Nothing more we can do for your mother. We're discharging her at noon today. She now needs palliative care.

She's on a continuous IV drip, I protested. She's had nothing to eat or drink since coming here. How will she survive? Where will she go?

She can go back to the retirement home now.

Back to the retirement home? I haven't spoken with the staff there. I didn't know Mom was going to be discharged. I thought you would look after her. I thought we could stay here until she gets better. She seems safe here. Will the retirement home accept her back? Will they be able to look after her? Please wait. I need to figure this out. I wasn't expecting this. Please not today.

I'm sorry, the social worker repeated, with deliberate finality, we're discharging your mother at noon today. She now needs palliative care. There's nothing more we can do for her here.

Palliative. I know the word but what does it mean? From the Latin, *palliare*, "to cloak; to prevent and relieve suffering, rather than to provide a cure."

Palliative: to cloak. How ominous that sounds. To cover the pain and suffering but not to heal. How will I conceal my pain and suffering?

Frantic now, I rushed out into the hallway to find the young doctor and ask again, Doctor, what is happening? Is Mom dying? What exactly is palliative care? I'm not sure the retirement home can provide it. I haven't been able to reach them to talk this over.

He responded matter of factly, Well, she's not actively dying. She still has all her vital signs. I'm sure the retirement home will be fine.

Not actively dying? I questioned. Angry now. Frustrated again by this inconclusive reply.

What does that mean? She hasn't been able to eat or drink. She's been on an IV drip for ten days. Please contact the resident doctor.

I remembered the senior resident from the time Mom was in the hospital nine years ago when she almost died of lithium toxicity. He was a kindly, older man. I was sure he would understand.

I rushed down the long gray-green hallway looking into every room, frantically trying to find him.

There he is. I'll hang around outside the door and wait. Oh no. I've just missed him.

He came out and headed in the opposite direction. I walked quickly to catch up. I wanted to run after him. I wanted to call out his name. Another doctor joined him and they continued down the corridor walking and talking animatedly.

I thought to myself, This is very embarrassing. Here I am practically stalking this man as if I were a teenager chasing a rock star for his autograph. I was screaming inside. I walked even faster. Breathless, I caught up and reached out for his arm.

Doctor, I have to talk to you. This is a matter of life and death. It's my mother. They want to discharge her. At noon. Today. She's on an IV. She's barely alive. How can I take her away? How can I look after her? She's safe here.

He stopped and looked at me. Quizzically. I was feeling like an idiot. I was probably not even making sense. What room is she in? he asked politely. I'll look at her file. I'll call a family conference for tomorrow morning.

I sighed with relief. He had given me a reprieve. One day's grace. Twenty-four hours.

That evening I went back to see Mom. What have they done? They have removed her IV. No, I called out. Who said you should do this? She will die.

The young doctor rebuked me, Calm down. I will check with the resident. He strode off down the hallway to the nursing station. He returned in a while. Yes, it was a mistake. I'll have it reinserted.

I watched. Mom's arm is swollen, red and bruised. The nurse can hardly find a vein for the IV. Too much is happening too quickly. I don't know what I should do. I don't know what I can do. I thought they would keep her here until she's better. Is there something they're not telling me? Do they think she's going to die? I don't really know what palliative care is and they haven't given me any specific directions. Am I in denial? Am I not understanding what they're saying, what they're trying to tell me?

If she is dying, they should be more direct. They should sit me down and say, Look, your Mom has not responded to the antibiotics. She is not eating or drinking on her own. While her vital signs are still evident we don't expect her to recover. Make the necessary arrangements to take her home or to a hospice.

But no one was saying that to me. All I was sure of was that she was safe here in this familiar hospital and she was in no state to be discharged anywhere.

Where should I take her? I asked myself. Who can look after her? Is palliative care the only solution? No one is telling me this directly. I don't even know what that really means— palliative care. All I know is they have shattered our safe quiet haven, our cocoon.

I have my daily routine
Here in this hospital room.
I come first thing in the morning.
I came back mid-afternoon.
I return in the evening when I can
Here to this hospital room.
I walk to the hospital gift shop.
I buy fresh flowers for Mom.
I get a mug of tea.
I hold her hands in mine.

I watch her breathe, softly, gently,
Maybe she will open her eyes.
Maybe she will speak to me.
Here in this hospital room.
Out! Out! They say.
No more to be done here.
Out of our safe quiet haven
Here in this hospital room.
I watch her breathe, softly, gently.
She is alive.
Still.

The next morning, the second day after they'd told us Mom was to be discharged, my brother and I met the senior resident in a small classroom in a hospital wing distant from Mom's room. We almost got lost trying to find it. We arrived breathless. We sat down on cold metal chairs. We felt as if we were in school again about to be reprimanded. The senior resident sat at the front of the room on one of the desks facing us. Two interns sat with him. One was familiar. I had spoken to her most recently about Mom. The other I didn't know. We began.

I explained what I knew. What they had told me.

They say the ten-day antibiotic cycle is complete.

They say there is nothing more they can do for Mom here.

They say they are discharging her at noon today. She has to go.

They are sending Mom back to the retirement home in a palliative state.

They have given me a pamphlet with a phone number to reach the palliative care team.

What should I do? I asked.

What do you say?

The resident doctor replied, Well, it's your decision. If she were my mother I'd want her out of here. Let her die quietly.

But the young intern says she's not actively dying.
And you say, I think you're saying, she is dying.

You say it's my decision, but everyone else here—the social worker, the community services person, the hospital discharge officer—they all say she has to go now. It doesn't feel as if it's my decision. It's their decision.

Why can't she stay here where she's safe in this familiar hospital? She's barely alive. She's only had intravenous fluids for ten days now. Can we take the IV with us? She's barely breathing. Please give me one more day. I need to understand so much. I have to learn so quickly how the system works.

The resident doctor graciously consented, One more day then. We'll discharge your mother tomorrow morning. Make the necessary arrangements.

Day twelve, the morning of the third day. It was now three days since the social worker's pronouncement that Mom was to be discharged. I had spent three days in shock and confusion trying to figure out what was best for Mom. I had been running around from one doctor to another begging them to let Mom stay in the hospital where she seemed so safe and secure.

I was standing in the hospital parking lot having a cell phone conversation with the palliative care team. A cold March wind was blowing my hair into my eyes. I had only just reached their office. The line was always busy.

I'm at the hospital now, I told the receptionist. My Mom is still here but they're discharging her back to her retirement home. They say she needs palliative care. What do you do? How can you help me?

The kindly voice answered me, When you get your mother settled in her room, ask the doctor there to call us and we can send someone over from the palliative team to help you. But we need a doctor's referral.

Thank you, I said, I'll do that. So that's it, I thought to myself. No more period of grace.

I made the hard decision to ask for the IV to be withdrawn knowing I was cutting off the fluids that had helped to sustain Mom. There was no turning back. I was taking her home to die. There was no other possible outcome.

I felt totally lost when I most needed support. Mom was dying. No one was telling me this directly. Death was imminent even if I refused to accept it. The medical team must have known. Why would no one tell me? Perhaps they had and I just refused to hear it. I was not yet ready to accept the truth.

Claudia Chowaniec

You're dying, Mom.
I guess I know.

I won't admit it,
not to myself,
not to my brother,
certainly not to you.

So many questions
I should have asked.
What keeps you going?
Are you thinking about death?
How can I bear this?

I'm sitting here beside you,
Beside your hospital bed.
My cheek against yours. So
warm, so soft, soft like a baby's.
You're going Mom and
you haven't told me
anything,
nothing at all,
since they brought you here.

I'm sitting here beside you.
Speak to me. Open your eyes.
Do you know I'm here?
I'm holding your hand.
Feel our hands touching?
I'm sure you can.

Nine years ago you were very sick.
They said you were dying. I sat beside
you just as I am now. I held your hand.
I cried a lot. Don't go, Mom. I knew
you wouldn't, even when they had me
sign the do not resuscitate document
and said I should call the pastor. I knew
you weren't going then. And you didn't.

But I know you are now and
I don't know if I can bear it.

8

It was noontime. Still day twelve. The next few hours were chaotic as I went through the procedures required to remove Mom from the hospital. I had finally reached the retirement home and confirmed that they could provide palliative care. That at least was a relief.

I went to the discharge office to arrange for transport back to the retirement home. I was told I had to pay in advance for this journey. I wanted to laugh. The incoming ambulance trip had been free; the outgoing trip required payment up front. In case there was no one left to pay? I was on the verge of hysteria.

The office suggested a company called Travois: "a rough log frame used by the Plains Indians to drag loads over land." An appropriate name. I certainly felt we were being dragged out of the hospital.

It was a familiar company. I used its services on special occasions to bring Mom to our house or to my brother's when she was in a wheelchair and no longer able to transfer to a car seat. I have a photo of Mom wearing the reindeer antlers' headband, which the good-natured French-Canadian Travois driver had jokingly put on Mom's head when she asked if she could have a hat like his. How strange then to be making this last journey in a vehicle we once called Mom's party delivery service. They let me sit in the back. I was holding Mom's hand.

Okay. I guess we're on our way out now, Mom.

No reply.

We arrived at the retirement home. Mom was wheeled out of the ambulance on the hospital gurney, through the front door, and down the long corridor to her room, the familiar room where she had lived for nine years. Back home.

She looked around. In an angry voice she said, This is all wrong. This is not home. I want to go home.

Mom, I said, we are home. Your familiar room. Back home.

I want to go home.

Where is home? I wondered. The home she'd raised us in where I grew up with my brother and our Dad? Or did she mean the home she'd been raised in? The faraway family home in Europe where she was born, where she played with her three brothers. The three brothers who teased her mercilessly as brothers do.

Where did Mom want to be in those moments so close to death? Where did she want to go? Somewhere else I did not know? Would she still tell me?

Mom was a deeply spiritual person who believed unquestioningly in the life hereafter. I knew she believed that after death she would be with her parents, her three brothers and her husband again. Could she see it? Could she imagine it? I was sure that was where she wanted to be even though I could not bear to let her go.

I believed it was Mom's faith that had carried her through the bitter sorrow of losing her brothers, her firstborn child, her parents and her husband; that supported her through her physical and mental illnesses; that enabled her to be joyful even as a frail old woman in a wheelchair, almost blind, nine years in one small room in a retirement home; that brought her finally to that moment of clarity and peace. I want to go home now. Her final words to me.

Where is home? I knew the answer, but the answer did not bring me comfort?

I understood, I couldn't yet come to terms with her dying. Did I share her beliefs? Would faith help me now? I had gone to Sunday School, been married in the church I grew up in, had my girls christened. But would my faith become in time as strong as hers and eventually comfort me and help me accept her dying and move on with my life? I did not yet know what I would have to go through before I achieved her sense of peace.

Mom's favorite nurse came in and together we settled Mom back in her familiar bed at the retirement home. I went to find the resident doctor. He was the man who had treated Mom over the last nine years for everything from bladder infections, to the bumps and bruises she suffered when she fell out of bed—before they put up the bed rails at night—to stomach flu and diarrhea when an epidemic swept through the home, to common colds and nosebleeds. He was the one who had arranged for me to take Mom to the local psychiatric hospital as a day patient when she was sure the devil was standing at the foot of her bed each morning waiting to drag her off to hell. He had come to know Mom well.

I asked him, Please tell me what is meant by palliative care.

He explained there are medications that are administered to the dying: to alleviate pain, to prevent the muscle spasms that occur as the body dehydrates, to keep the lungs from becoming congested.

But what will death be like? When will it come?

The body has an immense capacity to keep itself alive: five to seven days without water, ten to fourteen without food.

Mom told me that when she was a teenager she went without food and water for a few days. She was going to be a missionary and wanted to know what hunger and thirst would be like. We used to laugh and think what a strange idea. But you need your body, mind and spirit to want to be alive. Mom told me she did not want to live anymore. She told me, Do nothing more for me. Nothing.

But what will death be like?

The doctor said, Elderly people may go to the edge as a result of a medical crisis such as pneumonia, get a look beyond, and decide they do not want to come back.

I wasn't sure I could accept his view. I said, I don't understand what you mean—get a look beyond, decide not to come back. What did she see? Why would she want to leave us? Leave me? Leave me alone.

I returned to Mom's room. She was lying quite still in her own bed in that familiar place, with her shelf of religious books, her comfortable brown corduroy armchair, her plants on the small round coffee table by the window. Someone had kept them watered while we were away. I should thank them. The room was filled with light. Her green bed linens. Yellow-flowered nightdress. Her pale face. White hair.

Her nurse, Mom's favorite nurse, came in again. I asked her the difficult question that had been haunting me.

How will I know when she is dying? She lies so still. She does not open her eyes or move even her hands. Her body is warm and soft and alive. How will I know when she is dying? It's a gruesome question, but I am going to sit here by her bedside for most of the hours to come while she's still living. And I need to know. I need to prepare myself. I've never been with anyone who's dying before. I've never seen death.

She replied, The legs and feet will grow cold first and turn a faint bluish color. You'll see a pallor cross her face. We call it the shadow of death.

What does that mean: the shadow of death?

You'll see a gray-yellow color pass over her face. That's the shadow of death.

Mom's nurse was right. I did see this ominous shadow pass over Mom's face. Two times. It was a vivid physical and visual presence. Each time I was afraid. This was the moment and I was not ready. But each time it passed. Mom was still alive. She was not ready to leave me.

I went to see Mom's doctor again. He said gently, You must accept her dying. There is a stage at which you acknowledge your own imminent death: the acceptance stage.

I knew he was telling me this with good intentions to help me understand Mom was dying. But I wasn't ready to let her go. I wanted to ask her, Are you really at this stage? Are you ready to die? This concept of coming to a time in your life when you accept death is no comfort to me.

You lived your life hopefully despite so many hardships. You were always full of hope. And when your life brought you here—to dying—to the acceptance stage, are you really ready to go?

Nothing. Do nothing more for me. No to everything. I remembered you saying this to me. Not quietly, soft-spoken, as you usually were. You said it out loud, with a strong voice. You were ready!

I want to keep you
here with me.
Live Mom.
You must live.
Live.
I need you.

Don't go.

But I know
you have not changed
your mind. Your decision.
Your going.
Is it peace you want?
What is that?
Outside of life.
In death.

No more pain.
All those IVs.
All those surgeries.
All those shock treatments.

Nothing more.
No thing more.
You said that.
I understand that
now.

You want peace.
Free from all pain.
Free to see your loved ones
again.
Your decision to pass on
is your desire for peace.
I have to accept that.

But I do not,
I will not,

I cannot,
accept
death.

I want you
to stay
with me.

I put my hands against Mom's cheeks. I brushed back her hair with my fingers. I unfastened the top buttons of her nightdress. I folded back the cloth. I stroked her neck, the outline of her collar bones. Her skin was warm and soft. Soft and smooth. I lay my head on her bosom, gently, not all my weight. I did not want to waken her. She was sleeping so peacefully. I felt her breathing.

You're getting ready to leave me, Mom. I know it. I want to be ready. Will you speak to me? One last time. Will you hold my hand? I do not want to be afraid.

Saturday. It was only yesterday that we left the hospital to come back to the retirement home. I remembered thinking, I must be here when she dies. I must have this memory. It's important for both of us. Maybe my being here when she dies will somehow make up for Mom not being there when her parents died, when her husband died. That they died alone. That she will not.

The nurses slipped in quietly every few hours and moved her from one side to the other. They propped up pillows under her back. They brushed her hair and gently wiped her face and hands. They administered the drugs the doctor had prescribed. The ones he had told me about.

I showed them that I had learned at the hospital how to swab out her mouth with a little cold water. Be very careful, they warned me. Only moisten the sponge. You don't want her to choke.

I almost do want her to choke, I said to myself. I want her to wake up. Open her eyes. Sit up in bed. Why doesn't she move at all? Has her spirit already left her?

Staff members stopped by to see Mom: nurses' aides, housekeepers, and caregivers who had looked after her over the nine years she had been in the retirement home, and cooks and servers who remembered when she still came down to the dining room to have her meals. They came before work or at the end of their shift to ask how Mom was doing and to give me a hug.

Sunday. Two weeks since Mom was rushed to the hospital. My husband and I have called our daughters, and my brother and his wife, their sons, to come now. We brought sandwiches from home for lunch. We got coffee from the dining room at the retirement home. We were all together—the nine of us— since Dad died so long ago. Did Mom know we were there with her? She was lying so still, calm and peaceful. She did not seem to be in any pain.

I kept thinking, I am so afraid of her dying. What if she screams out? What if her body twists in agony? What can I do?

I remembered all those years ago when I sat with her, both of us crying when she received the news of her father's death. I felt so helpless to help her then, to relieve her pain. I have felt that way so many times. So helpless to help.

Her body continued to live, frail as it was, barely a hundred pounds. That body had been through so much and survived. Born during World War One in Europe. Little milk to be had. Lived through World War Two eating tulip bulbs when there was nothing else. That body had survived two bouts with cancer, breast and bladder, and electric shock treatments when she developed bipolar disease in mid-life. She had experienced lithium toxicity and her kidneys almost shut down before we knew what was wrong. Mom had survived all those traumas. Her body continued to live. No food, no water.

I remembered years ago after Dad died Mom had sent me a letter. She had written: My Funeral Arrangements on the front of the sealed envelope: Not to be opened until I die. I'd put it away but I was very curious to know what was in that note, so when Mom was critically ill nine years ago, I opened it.

She had written, I do not wish to have an open casket, which I know is the habit of your father's family. Face made up, waxen, unnatural, a death mask. People at the wake whispering, doesn't she look as if she were sleeping or she really looks much better than when I last saw her.

I would like to be cremated. I do not want to be buried in the dark, cold earth. You remember I told you once I had a terrible vision when I was putting in my first garden after the war. I saw my favorite brother's bones there in the earth among the bulbs and the roots. I could never garden again. I could not put my hands into that dark, cold earth. I was so afraid of what I might see.

When Mom recovered from her stroke and moved to the retirement home nine years ago, we sat down together one day at the round coffee table in her room near the window with all the flowering plants and we talked about her funeral arrangements.

Mom, I said, I agree, no open casket. But I don't like the idea of cremation. Dealing with the ashes seems so awkward, having to figure out where to keep them. I went with a friend once to scatter her mother's ashes and a wind blew up and they flew back in our faces. It was awful. I know it sounds old-fashioned but I'd like to think of you resting beside Dad in the family cemetery plot, if that's okay with you.

Yes, that's fine, she said, if that's what you would like.

We had our coffee together that day in the dining room at the home and chatted on about other family matters. I told her of some mischief I had gotten myself into as a teenager, along with my favorite cousin, at our aunt's funeral.

We were restless, I told Mom. We were bored by all the old folks who had gathered for the wake. We decided to explore the funeral home premises. Down in the basement we discovered the unlocked door to the coffin showroom. We looked at each other mischief on our minds. Irresistible.

My cousin taunted me, I dare you to get into one of the coffins.

I couldn't resist. I picked one I liked and slid down into it. So how do I look laid out in pink quilted silk?

His father, my uncle, came in just at that moment and yelled at us and sent us out with a stern warning, There's to be no more trouble from you two.

Mom laughed when I told her my story. The thought of funerals and making arrangements for her burial seemed unreal, so far in the future. I couldn't imagine it ever happening.

But now the time had come. There we were, my brother and I, on Monday morning at the retirement home together planning her funeral. Mom was in her bed dying. We were accepting that her death was imminent. We talked about the church service and the burial, the death announcement, who we should contact, the flowers. We agreed on the funeral home we would use. We made an appointment to go there in the afternoon.

The director greeted us solicitously solemn and ushered us formally into his office. He had prepared a list for us. He reviewed our options: cremation or burial, urn or coffin, open or closed, lead-lined or not. We decided: burial, coffin, closed, lead-lined. Then he invited us to view the coffins. He led us down the hallway to the showroom. There they were, lined up against three walls—rich lustrous mahogany and walnut, the most expensive; oak, shiny golden brown, less expensive; and the classic pine box with no brass ornamentation at all. There was also the latest environmentally green option—a heavy-duty recycled cardboard box. I had trouble suppressing my laughter. My brother thought I was at risk of becoming hysterical. But I was remembering the story I had told Mom about my mischievous cousin and I exploring a showroom very similar to this one and I had been caught modeling how I would look in a coffin. I had never told my brother the story. We chose the oak coffin, simple, tasteful. Our mother always liked oak furniture.

So the funeral arrangements were sorted out, now the burial plans. Another bizarre memory came to mind.

Almost fifty years ago our parents bought a double plot in a cemetery out in the country close to the town where we grew up. I still remembered the cemetery salesman. I'd just come in from a high school basketball game, tired and hungry, and looking forward to dinner, and there was this man, the burial plot salesman, sitting at our dining room table. No meal in sight. He had oily black slicked-back hair, a persuasive voice, and a shiny dark suit a little tight for his large frame. He was showing my parents a map of the cemetery. They were trying to decide which plots to buy. There were several sections to choose from.

I leaned over to take a look and in a dreadfully sarcastic voice I remember saying, Really don't choose the Ten Commandments section, too rigid. I think you should go for the Last Supper area, you can count on some bread and wine before you go. Silly thing to say really.

The salesman ignored me as did my parents. Now, he said, how would you like to pay for your new site? We have a monthly installment program you might be interested in.

I had been annoyed with my parents that long ago evening. I told them, I really can't believe you're thinking about buying cemetery plots now. And by installments. It'll be years before you'll need them. I went off to the kitchen to make myself a peanut butter sandwich.

That was fifty years ago. I was just a kid starting high school. Death. Burial. Unimaginable events. And there I was in my home office going through old files looking for those documents. Mom gave them to me for safe keeping after Dad died. I phoned the cemetery. The administrator told me the plot was fully paid for, of course, on the installment plan, and the name plates as well. But there were additional expenses, she explained, for the transportation of the body, and the opening and closing of the site as they tastefully described it.

I spent Tuesday sitting by Mom's bedside. Wednesday was April Fool's Day, the day before Mom's birthday. I always tried to trick Mom but she only fell for my jokes once. I put sugar into the salt shaker. What a face she made when she sprinkled it on her soft-boiled egg that long ago morning. She told me that when she was born her mother had been anxious that she not arrive on the first of April.

My brother and I spent Wednesday evening with Mom, sitting by her bedside, quietly talking. I reminded him how much fun Mom always made our birthdays when we were young. I told him, For me the biggest birthday treat was eating Mom's homemade cake for breakfast even on school days when she usually made sure we had a healthy meal. That was her special way of celebrating. Of course, she did the same for your birthday. But you were just a kid, I teased him. Can you remember? I remember she would light the birthday candles and get you and Dad to carry a bouquet of flowers and the cards and gifts. I would hear you tromping up the stairs to my bedroom. I was so excited but I would pretend I was still asleep. She would quietly open my bedroom door and begin singing "Happy Birthday" in her melodious voice, followed by a pre-selected hymn. I would sit up in bed, blow out the candles, and open the presents and envelopes. Then we would all go downstairs to the kitchen and eat birthday cake. You and Dad got the same treatment but we never managed it for Mom. She was always up too early in the morning.

On Thursday, April 2, shortly after midnight, we said, Happy Birthday, Mom. My brother and I hugged each other and went home.

In the morning I returned with an enormous bouquet of red tulips to silently celebrate her birthday. I sat by her bed and watched her breathe, softly, gently, moment by moment.

Two nurses came in to keep watch with me. We kept watch together. Mom's favorite nurses. The three of us sitting by her bed watching her breathe. One breath. Then another. She was so peaceful. She was breathing very gently, one breath, and then another, so softly I could barely hear it. She was so peaceful.

One breath. Then another. And then no breath at all.

Graceful, peaceful, quiet death. In the midst of my busy, sometimes chaotic life, she left me. Alone.

Mom taught me so much about life.

Now this is her final lesson to me.
There is no fear in dying.

Do not fear my dying.
I am ready to go.
I want to go home.
Thank you for all the love
You have given me.

Do not fear my dying.
I am ready to go.
I want to go home now.

As for me,
I will know death when I am dying
And I will not be afraid.

Thursday, April 2 at 10 AM, Mom's ninety-fourth birthday, she slipped away ever so quietly on that bright and sunny spring morning. I always thought the words passed away were just a nicer way of saying died. But no, passed away was exactly right.

Mom has just died.
How can this be?
Her birth day.
Her death day.

No need to mark today
The day you died.
It is your birthday.
It will always be your birthday.

Birth day
Death day.
The day you died.

It is your birthday.
I cannot celebrate
The day you died.
I mourn.
In time
I hope
To celebrate.

I got up from the chair beside Mom's bed, steeling myself to face the hardest days of my life. The nurses left Mom's room to call the coroner to sign the death certificate and the funeral home to take away her body and prepare it for burial. I left to call my brother and my husband and daughters.

9

As I was walking back along the corridor to Mom's room I heard a strong voice singing. I opened the door. The cook, a robust black lady, was standing at the foot of Mom's bed, singing "Rock of Ages," Mom's favorite. Then she sang a rousing "Happy Birthday." I hugged her. I explained, I'm so sorry. Mom has just died.

No, that's not possible, she said. Your Mom looks so peaceful. She looks just as she did yesterday when I sang to her. I've done that every morning before I start work. I'm late this morning.

We stood there together tears streaming down our faces.

When does death actually occur? I wondered. Had she really been alive all those days when she did not move, when she did not say a word, when she gave no indication she was aware of my presence, when only her breathing marked her alive? Was she sleeping? Was she already gone?

But she did wait for me. She did not die in the night. She did not die early this morning. She waited for me to be with her, to hold her hand, to let her go. She wanted me to be with her.

She wanted me to know there is no fear in death.

My brother arrived. We sat quietly together beside Mom's bed. She passed away very peacefully, I whispered. She was breathing and then she was not. Very, very peacefully.

The coroner arrived to formalize her death. The man from the funeral home arrived to take her body away. My brother and I left her room and waited in the hall. Mom's favorite nurse came to offer her condolences. The door reopened. Mom was lying on a wheeled stretcher covered with a white sheet. The man pushed the stretcher out the door and down the long corridor. We walked behind her, the three of us, Mom's favorite nurse, my brother, and me, arm in arm, supporting each other. Back the way we had come only six days ago, out to the waiting hearse. We watched it drive away and then we went home.

The funeral service would be in the morning, day after tomorrow. We would arrange for our girls to fly home, for my brother's boys to come. We would contact the minister who would conduct the memorial service, our relatives and Mom's few remaining friends. We would send the obituary we had already written to our local newspaper. We would buy food for the get-together of family and close friends after the funeral as was expected. We would confirm that the burial would be the morning after the funeral.

The death announcement would read: She was survived by her daughter and her son, their spouses, and four grandchildren. She was predeceased by her husband seventeen years ago. She was laid to rest in the family plot in Roselawn Memorial Gardens, the Last Supper section.

All this lay ahead for me to take care of. The next steps. Could I do it? No choice. These were the familiar rituals of our culture to honor Mom's passing. These were the death rites our family and friends expected. I had been through all this when Dad died, but then there'd been Mom to be comforted and to comfort me. We were mother and daughter. Now my mother was gone. Could I still be a daughter even with no mother? I wondered.

Who am I now?
No longer a daughter.
Mom passed away.
Who am I now?
I am not sure.

Did I come to think of daughter as my most important role? Why is that? Was being daughter the role that brought the most satisfaction? Caring, helping, supporting.

What about mother? Wife? I guess they don't need me as much—anymore.

Rebuild my life.
Find a new role.
No longer a daughter.
Mom passed away.

Who am I now?
Oldest in the family.
Next in line to die.
Reflection on my mortality.

Who am I now?
Still mother, spouse,
sister, aunt, cousin.

Who might I become?
The wise old woman of the family.
The one who carries on the traditions.
The one who records the family history.
The one who writes about Mom.
The legacy builder.
An honorable role from ancient time.

Part 2

Mourning Mom

10

Palm Sunday. Early morning. Four days ago Mom died. Two days ago we held her funeral. One day ago—just yesterday—we buried her in the cold black earth of a rainy early spring morning. All those days had gone by.

I had not written a word in my journal since Mom died. I was numb with grief. Mom was dead. She was gone. What comfort would my journaling bring me now? What would I write? What difference would it make?

Then last night I dreamed of Mom.

I'm with a group of friends: happy, laughing and talking. I look up and there's Mom waiting down the road. She waves. I wave back excited and shout, There's my Mom. I run as fast as I can into her arms. We hug each other. I don't want to let her go. My friends catch up. This is my Mom. I want to introduce them but I can't remember my friends' names. We stand there for a while, happy, laughing, and talking. Mom has bright copper hair the color it was when she was a girl. I know because I once found a large curl she had cut off and put in a box as a keepsake. She's conversing animatedly but I can't hear what she's saying.

I woke up excited. I saw Mom. I have been longing for this. I did have a brief dark dream the night after she died and it was full of pain. She was in her wheelchair and we were crying. I did not want to put that in my journal. I did not want to write about my deep sorrow.

Why was that? Why didn't I want to reflect on my unbearable sorrow in the midst of experiencing it? Perhaps it was an instinct. Perhaps it was necessary for survival. Perhaps it was what Mom did throughout her life to deal with all the grief and loss she had to face. Push it away, down, out of her consciousness. Perhaps this was one of her secrets to finding a peaceful life despite all the pain she had to face.

But when I remembered my dream about Mom all my doubts about keeping up my journal faded away. I thought, perhaps it is only through writing about Mom that I can keep her memory alive, keep her presence with me. I have to keep on writing to keep her near me.

At the same time, I reflected, if I am going to continue writing in my journal, writing about Mom and all we shared, and if my writing is to support and comfort me in my mourning, if it is to help me understand how she lived her life and found peace, then I will have to confront my deep sorrow through my writing and learn to express it honestly and directly. Only then will I be able to find my way forward to a new stage of my life and arrive in time at a place of renewal and hope.

On that Palm Sunday morning when I woke up with the dream of Mom still so tangible in my memory, I thought how different my experience had been when Dad passed away all those years ago. I had dreamed of him vividly the first night after his death—a heart attack on a cold and miserable early March morning. I was not there with him. No one was.

That was a long time ago. I don't think I felt the same deep sorrow or immense sense of loss when Dad died. Was that because I never became his caregiver? Our lives were never so intertwined.

After the funeral home took Mom's body away, my brother and I returned to our own homes for a few hours. I phoned my husband and our daughters—Mom has passed on.

My husband said, I'll get flights for the girls. Are you all right? he asked. What does he mean? I thought. No. Nothing is right, or ever will be again. Mom is dead.

My brother and I returned to Mom's room in the retirement home later on that same afternoon to divide up the tasks that came next.

It was still Wednesday. Still the day Mom died. I shook my head in disbelief. It could not be. I sat down at Mom's desk. I held my head in my hands. I had to do this. I called the funeral home first.

Please bring in her clothes—her best outfit and her shoes.

Her shoes. Are you sure? The coffin will be closed.

Yes, the funeral home director continued, and any religious symbol you would like her to wear—a cross, perhaps, or a rosary. We will dress her and make up her face so she will look just as she always did.

How could you possibly know how she looked? I wanted to say, full of life and hope, her welcoming smile, her sense of peacefulness.

I remembered my father's death all those years ago. He was laid out in a white-quilted satin-lined oak coffin, open to the waist, in our town's one and only funeral home. The undertaker had dressed him in his navy blue blazer with the embroidered Cameron Highlanders military crest on his breast pocket, a starched white shirt, and his regimental tie: navy, maroon and green diagonal stripes. He had worn that same outfit at my wedding nineteen years earlier. A little too much rouge and powder to look natural but he did look peaceful. I could have reached out to touch him. I could have kissed him but I did not. I never got to say good-bye. I was away on holidays, with my husband and our two daughters, skiing on March break. My brother had called me.

Dad died, he said, a heart attack. Someone noticed him in the shopping center parking lot this morning slumped over the steering wheel. You'd better come right away.

I did. I came immediately that day all those years ago as I should have done when I heard Mom had been taken to the hospital. Guilt remained ever present.

More memories of Dad's funeral came to mind. I recalled how much Mom had hated the idea of the open casket, but it was what Dad wanted, what our family expected. The three of us—Mom, my brother and I—made all the arrangements with the funeral home for a wake to be held the afternoon and evening before the funeral. Family members, neighbors and friends came to express their condolences. People I hadn't seen for many years.

I wondered even then, is there something cathartic about going to a funeral? Perhaps we're relieved deep down inside that it's someone else this time. Perhaps we need to share in the grieving because we reflect on our own mortality and acknowledge our time will come too.

Our older daughter was eleven when Dad died. He had given her his Cameron Highlanders cap pin because even then she had a great interest in military history. She would beg her grandfather to tell her war stories. And he did. Many tales of his World War Two experiences.

At the funeral she insisted on wearing the heavy silver pin on her blue woolen cardigan. I'm wearing this for Opa, she said to her sister, proudly pointing to it. He gave it to me. He would want me to wear it today.

An army colleague of Dad's overheard her. He said to our younger daughter, who was eight, Would you like to have a silver pin like your sister's? I have one too just like your grandfather's. We served together. He was a brave soldier. My son has no interest in these things and I have no one else to give it to. I will send it to you if you would like it.

Seventeen years ago. I rubbed my hand along the worn edge of Mom's desk as I sat there in her room remembering. I have to stop this—all my memories of Dad's funeral. I have to focus on the arrangements for Mom's. I continued my phone conversation with the funeral home director.

The next question he asked, Would you like to visit your Mom one last time?

No thank you.

I believed Mom and I had taken our leave of each other that day in the hospital when she had suddenly awakened from her coma-like state for just a moment and said, Thank you for all you have done for me, for all your loving care. I want to go home. Do not do anything more for me. Nothing. No thing. I didn't know it then but I did now. She had given me her blessing. That was our good-bye.

What about your daughters? he continued.

No thank you.

I was quite sure they would not want to see their Oma lying in her coffin, with her confirmation cross around her neck, dressed up in her best clothes, including her shoes. But I did ask them two days later, when we were getting dressed in our black outfits for the funeral, Did I make the right decision?

Yes, for sure, Mom, our elder daughter reassured me. I hugged Oma good-bye before I went back home after Christmas. I didn't know it would be for the last time, but she made me promise, Look after your Mom. I thought it was a strange thing to say. But, you know, I was in a rush and didn't give it a second thought.

Our younger daughter reminded me, You remember when we visited Oma at Christmas. My friend took that photo of our hands intertwined. When I showed it to her, she said, How lovely. I will treasure this. We hugged and she looked at me with tears in her eyes. I think she knew we would never be together again.

Next on my list, I called the minister to confirm her availability and the time for the funeral on Friday. We talked over the program, what hymns, what Bible readings, who would say what, what she would say. She was new to our church and had never met Mom.

So many details, I thought. No time to cry. Get on with my list of things to do. Strange comfort.

But I couldn't get the memories of Dad's funeral out of my head. How complicated those arrangements had been.

When Dad died my parents were still living in our home town in the house my brother and I grew up in. We'd been going to the same church for thirty-five years. I'd been married there. But Dad didn't like the new minister who had come ten years before. They'd had an argument early on about the interpretation of some biblical passages.

I remembered Dad saying to Mom, I don't want that man to bury me. And Mom, angry, replied, I don't want to talk about this: your dying, your funeral, your dislike of our minister. You know I like his sermons. Mom and Dad seldom argued mainly because Mom rarely challenged him, but when it came to religion she made her stand.

The day after Dad died Mom and I were going through his chest of drawers, looking for socks and underwear to take to the funeral home along with the rest of his clothes, and we

95

found the note he'd left for her: My Funeral Arrangements, saying explicitly that he did not want that minister to conduct his funeral.

Mom was upset. What are we going to do? I can't imagine not having the funeral in our church. You know I like the minister and everyone will expect us to have it there.

In the end, to keep the peace, Mom agreed to hold Dad's service in the funeral home chapel. But she was very distressed by that arrangement for a long time afterward.

Get back to the present, I chided myself. It was still Wednesday late afternoon. Still so much to be done. I opened the center drawer of Mom's desk and took out her small red leather address book. I turned the pages. Who should I call? We did this together, Mom and I, every Christmas. Who should we call to wish them "Happy Holidays" and say we're thinking of you and hope you have a good year ahead? So many names crossed off. So few left to contact.

On Thursday morning I made the death announcement cards, which we handed out at the funeral. I hadn't liked the ones the funeral home offered us so I decided to make them myself. I got out Mom's wedding album. We used to love looking through it together. One of our favorite photos was of Mom and Dad coming out of the church, just married. A little boy is running in front of them, through the crowd, down the sidewalk, where Dad's jeep is waiting. He was the ring bearer, the son of the neighbor who had directed Dad to Mom's house when he was looking for a room to rent that day of jubilant celebrations when the Canadians liberated Holland.

For the front of the card I chose the formal photo of Mom's engagement. She was already wearing her wedding dress, dark brown velvet, beautifully tailored, fitted waist, falling elegantly in bias-cut panels to the floor. She had it made from her living room drapes. There was no white fabric available in occupied Holland at the end of World War Two, not even from the black marketers. She was holding a bouquet of calla lilies. Waxy white. Radiant. Such an overworked word, the radiant bride to be, but it was the word that best fit that moment. For the inside of the card I picked a photo of our lake, the view from Mom's cottage bedroom window. She loved being there, peaceful and quiet, out in nature.

The previous day I had purchased blank cards to use for the death announcement. But it took me some time to figure out how to print the cards from my computer so that the photos and the text came out right side up on the inside and the outside.

In the late afternoon I went to the airport to pick up our two daughters. They had been here last Sunday before their Oma died and then returned home to their distant cities. They had hugged her and repeatedly spoken her name and held her hands, just as I had done those last dreadful days in the hospital. But Mom lay silent still not answering. I tried to assure them that somehow she did know they were there with her, saying their good-byes.

I parked near the edge of the airport lot and got out of the car. I wondered how I was going to be a bit upbeat in welcoming my girls home. In the darkening blue light of early April a robin was singing loudly and cheerfully. The first one I'd heard this spring. As the three of us walked back to the car arm in arm we could hear it still singing. We went to look. There it was in a leaf bare tree in the dark blue night. Singing. For us.

We ordered pizza for supper that evening. No one to bring in food as they used to do. I recalled that when someone died neighbors, family and friends would stop by the house with homemade casseroles, freshly baked buns, and cakes and cookies. It was almost celebratory. So many visitors. All the food. Eating and drinking too. Get-togethers after the wake, after the funeral. These gatherings were often quite boisterous in our big Irish-Scottish family. As a young adult I had enjoyed these events: reunions with aunts, uncles and cousins that only seemed to happen at weddings and funerals.

My brother and I decided we would not hold a wake for Mom. There were too few family members left to have a visitation at the funeral home before the church service and I hadn't told anyone else, only our closest friends. Nevertheless, this change in ritual disturbed me immensely. I wanted our relatives, neighbors and friends to bring food to our house to share with us. I wanted them to express their condolences and to hug and cry together. I wanted them to acknowledge that Mom had passed on, that we had begun to mourn.

Friday was the funeral. We dressed formally in black, self-conscious, as if in costume. The eight of us: my brother and me, our spouses, and our kids. We entered the church in procession following the coffin down the center aisle. I nodded a greeting to family and friends as we passed. I was glad for a moment that they were there to support us. We sat down in the front row facing Mom's coffin. Tears were streaming down my face. I couldn't stop them. My daughters were on either side of me sitting arm in arm and passing me dry tissues as mine got soggy.

After the funeral service we went downstairs to the church hall where we greeted the people who came and served them tea and coffee. We invited everyone to join us for refreshments at our home a few blocks away. But only our small family and a few close friends came over. We had lunch. Not much drinking. A glass or two of wine.

I had hoped my cousin would show up, the mischievous one I had played with in the funeral home coffin sales room more than fifty years ago. I hadn't seen him since his own father had passed away five years ago.

Saturday. The day of the burial. Cold, windy, rainy early April. The cemetery was out in the country, halfway between our home town and the city where my brother and I lived now. I'd only been there once since Dad died.

When my parents were alive we would visit the family graves at least once a year, usually on Mother's or Father's Day. Mom told us that in Europe on November 1—All Saints Day, and November 2—All Souls Day, the cemeteries would be alive at night with mourners who lit flickering red candles to mark the tombs of their loved ones.

The chaos of memories of deaths, funerals and cemeteries closed in around me. I thought of my parents-in-law too. My husband and I had not visited their graves since their deaths several years ago.

Claudia Chowaniec

I remembered a poem I had written after visiting the cemetery
in Lviv, Ukraine, the city once known as Lvov, when it was still
part of prewar Poland, the city where my parents-in-law had
been born.

Lvov ancient city once Poland
War moved to another land
Your great cemetery
City of the dead
Through tall black gates
Arched over darkness
All Saints and All Souls

Foreign to the living
Great city of the dead
Rising on undulating hills
Shadowed landscape flickering red
Candlelight in the night mist
All Saints and All Souls
Monuments towering on high land
Great stone angels and ornate crosses
Statues of saints and heroes
Valleys of modest graves
Slabs resting on cold ground.

We bring candles for black graves
none have remembered.
We search names
looking for connections.
But find none
On this celebratory
night of the dead.

There we were at the cemetery to bury Mom. We followed the pall bearers carrying Mom's coffin to the grave site. Shivering in the icy rain. Slipping in the mud. Two bronze plaques were set into the ground. No granite head stone. Dad's marked with his birth date, his death date. Mom's just her birth date. Death too recent to be recorded.

Just the eight of us gathered together in the cold rain around Mom's coffin resting on a green baize cloth that covered the grave opening. The harsh wind pulled a rose from the bouquet we had brought from the church. I reached down to pick it up.

As we were leaving a young cousin pulled up in his truck and his three kids ran over to give me a hug. They had visited Mom last year on her ninety-third birthday and had brought her handmade cards, which she kept for a while on her round coffee table by the window. She had made a big fuss over the children and offered them a box of chocolate-covered caramels the retirement home staff had given her for her birthday.

I'm sure I'll never eat them, she said. They stick to my teeth. You have them. Take them home with you. Don't eat them all at once.

My cousin brought me a photo. Mom and Dad's wedding day. I thought you might like this, he said, not quite sure of the appropriate words of condolence. I found it in Grandma's album. Maybe you don't have this one.

His grandmother was Dad's oldest sister. She had given Mom and Dad a room when Mom first arrived as a war bride.

He held out the photo for me to see.

I don't have this one, I said. It's lovely. Thank you so much for bringing it. I quickly put it in my purse before the rain spattered the old photo. I thanked him with all my heart. He was the only one who had made the journey to be with us in this lonely place.

My brother and I had performed the rituals to honor Mom's passing the way our family had always dealt with death: the funeral arrangements, the church service, the invitation to come back to the house for refreshments, the grave-site visit. These familiar rites had comforted family members and closest friends who'd gathered to offer each other solacing words and hugs as they mourned.

All the funerals and all the burials I had attended of grandparents, aunts and uncles, parents-in-law, Dad. All those deaths should have prepared me in some way for mourning Mom. But they did not. I did not know how I would live through this dark cloud of sorrow.

On Palm Sunday the day after Mom's burial I went to the church Mom and I had attended regularly. I thought it would be comforting to continue our Sunday routine. That I might feel Mom's presence there. But it was painful. People asked, How are you? We haven't seen you for a few weeks. How's your mother? I had to answer, She passed away four days ago. We buried her yesterday. Please don't ask me, How are you? I'll cry when I tell you how much I miss her. I knew they meant well. But after that church experience I chose, consciously or unconsciously, not to tell anyone Mom died. I couldn't bear losing her.

11

It was the Monday after Palm Sunday and life continued on. My daughters traveled back to their homes and my husband went to work. But I didn't know how I was going to get through one hour to the next, from Monday to Tuesday, and then all the days that would follow.

Seconds, minutes pass
Then hours, days, nights.

Clocks confuse, distort,
fail to mark the passing
time stands still.
Minutes hours days
Time races on.

Clock's
face
my face,
all my tears.

The first days after Mom's death. Get up. Eat. Work. Go to bed. My daily routine. My round blue-edged clock on the kitchen wall ticked loudly. It was Mom's. She had it beside her bed so she could keep track of what was happening in her day. As long as she could see the hands. As long as she cared about the passing of time.

Breakfast, I stand at the counter. My bowl of oatmeal. Add flaxseed. Add dried blueberries. Add boiling water. Add up the minutes. Add up the hours. Add a day. Add a night. Add another day. My daily routine. Add a meeting, add an appointment, add grocery shopping, add the meals my husband and I share, add up the hours, add a night, add another day, my busy agenda, keep it filled, keep me going.

My daily routine, my new routine, my work a relief caught up in routine. No visits to Mom. How would I spend those extra hours in my daily agenda? The day just past. This day. The day to come. All those days went by in a cold gray empty fog that caught me up and moved me on day after day.

Minutes, hours, days passed. How are you doing? they asked. Do they really want to know? Fine. I'm fine, I said. Do they really want me to tell them? I cry all day. I cry all night. Should I tell them? Morning, I wake up with a start, relieved to be in my own bed. How did I get here? Did I sleep? I do not remember. Evening, what did I do all day?

Wednesdays and Sundays were the hardest to get through. The two days I spent with Mom, almost without exception, for the nine years she was in the retirement home. Almost five hundred Wednesdays and Sundays.

I remembered the last Wednesday service in the retirement home chapel the week before Mom died. Two nursing students from Nigeria sang a rousing gospel hymn with a joyful spirit, "Just one more time, we'll pray together. Just one more time we'll sing together. Just one more time we'll stay together." And now all those times are past.

Those visits were a part of my life, my weekly agenda, my routine. I wanted it back. My daily routine with Mom. I wanted Mom back.

12

Should I wear black as Mom did when she was in mourning? I opened my closet. I had a lot of black clothes.

Mom had often told me, You really don't look good in black. It's not a color for a young woman.

Mom, I'm not that young anymore.

I had to wear black for a year after my father died, she said, and then for many more months after my mother died. I hate the color. It makes me think of death.

I know Mom, I said. I remember going with you to buy clothes. You bought a necklace made of black jet, cut like the crystals of a chandelier, and a sleeveless black dress. And you had a warmer one too with long sleeves. Everything you wore for more than a year was black—hat, gloves, stockings, shoes. I complained, Why can't you put on your flowered green dress? It's my favorite, Mom. I hate you wearing black all the time.

In those days when Mom wore black it was a sign in the community. She was in mourning. It allowed her, perhaps even permitted her, to grieve in public. Neighbors and friends would ask, How are you doing? And listen to her response. And say some comforting words. People did that. They knew what to do. They reached out to her and she was comforted.

I wore black each day that spring after Mom's death and into the early summer months. But no one seemed to associate my wearing black with my grieving. No one asked me, Are you in mourning? I'm so sorry for your loss. Is there anything I can do to help?

Why doesn't our culture today, in any case, our North American culture, provide me with any accepted guidelines for expressing my grief in public? I kept asking myself, Are we afraid to acknowledge our mortality? Are we sheltered from death, from watching the slow withering away of aging loved ones who, a generation ago, would have lived with their children when they could no longer manage on their own? Do we plan funerals to avoid confrontation with the reality of death? Cremation, a private family gathering, a memorial service with personal stories to share. If we go to the cemetery, the casket is frequently left discretely on the surface, the hole neatly covered from view, so we can avoid the hollow thudding of earth shoveled down on the wooden box lowered into the ground. We walk away. Someone else will finish the work of burying our dead.

For me, the language and rituals of death were familiar from childhood. *Laid out:* the corpse in an open coffin, the face made up, life-like as a doll, dressed in Sunday best clothes, arms folded peacefully across the chest, hands clasping a treasured rosary or cross. *Visitation of the deceased:* often at home in the front room or in the funeral parlor. *Wake:* the respectful gathering of family and friends after the funeral and burial. In my father's family, in the old Irish-Scottish tradition, that often included a party. *Internment:* the lowering of the casket into a gaping hole in the ground, with the pastor or priest intoning the grim words, "ashes to ashes, dust to dust."

I could still remember in vivid multisensory detail my earliest experiences of death and funerals. Two occasions, in particular.

The first. I'm six years old. A dear old aunt is laid out in her coffin in her own home. I walk into the familiar front room, sharp intake of breath, the powerful fragrance of incense—strange and exotic. Candles flickering in red glass containers. Soft weeping, whispering, shushing of the children's voices. Soft touch of the shiny white silk lining. Hard-polished surface of the casket.

I know instinctively I should not reach out to touch the smooth soft face of my aunt or her thin lined hands clasped around the black jet beads of her rosary. But I really want to. She lies there so still. I do not understand.

The second. My school friend. I witnessed his death. Right before my eyes. More than fifty years ago. I have pushed this image away many times. But it was as vivid as the moment it happened.

It's just after lunch, winter, overcast, slightly warming because the roads are slushy. I'm seven in grade two and excited to be out of school on an excursion to a classical music concert in our small town's high school auditorium. We had to pay a quarter for the ticket and only a few of my classmates are going. The rest are still back at school. It's a long walk and we're playing in the snow along the way. My best friend smashes a snowball into my neck and then dashes away to get out of range of my return throw. I chase after him. Into the street. I trip over a snowbank and fall in the dirty wet snow. A screech of brakes. A soft thud. He's lying down. Not moving. Blood on his face.

I stand up desperately trying to brush the muddy slush off my new winter coat with its soft gray fake fur collar. My white-ribbed cotton stockings are dirty and wet. I want to go to the concert. I can't go like this. I'm crying. An ambulance arrives and my schoolmate is gently lifted onto a stretcher. The teachers decide we should continue on. I remember sitting on a hard metal chair at the concert and not really liking the music. The next morning the principal comes in to our class and tells us my friend died. Dead? Do I know what that means? We were just playing.

I'm at his funeral. An open coffin. His forehead is wrapped in white bandages. He's wearing a suit. His face is calm. He truly looks asleep.

I still don't know how to make sense of this even now. My friend. We were playing and then he was gone. It could have been me.

I recognized that the ritual of the funeral, familiar since childhood, was a way to say good-bye. But with Mom's passing I came to realize it was only the beginning, the beginning of my mourning. I would have to find my own way to lay my memories to rest, to get me to a new place in my life, beyond the overwhelming sorrow. I hoped my writing would help me. But I didn't know how I was going to make that journey through grief and loss to renewal.

13

Brilliant blue
Unexpectedly warm
Easter Sunday morning.

Past your birthday
Past your death day
Easter Sunday morning.

I'm not dyeing
Easter eggs this year.
Why bother.
You're dead.
The kids are away.
Easter Sunday morning.

The sky is brilliant blue.
The air unexpectedly warm
For such an early April day.
Easter Sunday morning.

I find
A piece of broken egg shell
Lying on the ground.

Robin's egg
Robin egg blue
Easter eggs
Robin egg blue

I will dye
Easter eggs
Robin egg blue

Not for you
Anymore.
For me.
Easter Sunday morning.

Eight days had passed since Mom's burial. Nine since her funeral. Eleven since her death. How did I get to here? To this celebratory day on the calendar, a green hill rising unexpectedly out of the dull gray mist of the passing days. Remembering Mom's love of celebrations. Remembering to remember. Easter. Coloring the eggs, hiding them, searching for them, eating them together around the breakfast table. Remembering to remember.

I remembered our annual conversation. Mom calls to ask, Have you been saving onion skins to use to dye the Easter eggs? It's only a few weeks until Easter. Your father and I don't eat many onions these days so I don't have enough.

No, Mom, I forgot. I'll save them from now on until you come. I promise.

I remembered our Easter ritual. From my childhood. Carried on with my daughters.

We hard boil the eggs in a big pot of water with the onion skins and they turn a deep russet brown. This is a tradition from the old country when there were no commercial Easter egg dyes. We add the novelty of writing a message or a name on the eggs in white crayon before immersing them in the boiling water and, like magic, it seems, the words are visible on the eggs when we remove them from the pot. We dry them and place them in brightly colored Easter baskets lined with shredded green paper grass.

When our two girls were still young I would get up early in the morning before anyone else to hide the candy and chocolates in the backyard. Sometimes in snowbanks, if spring was late. Sometimes under the new green leaves of the evergreen plants—the pachysandra and periwinkle, and the low-growing juniper bushes. One year the squirrels found them first. The next year I bought brightly colored hollow plastic eggs and filled them to safeguard the treats.

I have a photo I took on Easter quite a few years ago. We're all together: Mom, Dad, my brother and his wife, their two boys, our two girls, my husband and me, the whole family, the ten of us in our Sunday best standing beside the big spruce tree in our front yard. Our younger daughter is bare-legged. I had to peel off her muddy white cotton-ribbed stockings before I could take that photo. She tripped and fell while hunting for eggs in our backyard, trying hard in competition with her sister to collect the most.

I did try that Sunday morning less than two weeks after Mom's passing to continue our Easter rituals. I dyed the eggs myself as we had always done together, but it was so hard. All my memories of Mom and all we had shared were on my mind and I had that deep down it-can-never-be-the-same-again feeling.

Mom had loved celebrations. Could I keep up those rituals? I wasn't a good baker or cook as Mom had been. No green-iced cupcakes for St. Pat's. No heart-shaped chocolate cake, with white icing and cinnamon candies, even though I now had those Valentine's baking tins. But dyeing Easter eggs—that I could do.

I invited my brother and his wife and boys to join my husband and me for Easter lunch. It was what we always used to do. Our daughters weren't coming. They lived too far away. But later on that day each of them called to tell me they had dyed eggs too, not just in honor of their Oma's memory, but because it was fun and had become part of their Easter tradition too. They would share this with me now. This was a ritual we would keep. That consoled me immensely.

14

I considered again the question I had asked myself after Mom's passing, When does death actually occur? From a medical perspective it was about the body's vital signs, whether the heart was still beating, the lungs functioning, the brain active. I recalled Mom's last days in the retirement home after we brought her back from the hospital. She had said to me, This is not home. Those were her final words. She didn't speak to me again. She didn't reach out to touch my hand. She lay quite still, peacefully still until she stopped breathing on that bright and sunny spring morning.

Her birthday. Her death day. Had her spirit already left her body sometime earlier? Or had she waited to die until I was there with her that morning? How can I ever know the answer to any of my questions about death? Mom's death, Mom's life?

Even before Mom's passing, I had been troubled by so many unanswered questions. I was sitting by her deathbed one afternoon trying to concentrate on reading a book, Sara Greun's *Water for Elephants*.

The author's narrator is candid and cranky, with a sharp twist of black humor. Am I ninety or ninety-three? I don't know, he complains. Or do I just not want to remember? He describes his own frailties and his frustrations and annoyances about the characters who share the constricted world of the retirement home he now inhabits. They're all so old. They're all so helpless, he says. Why am I here? I'm not ready to be here.[1]

I remembered that I put the book down and said, Wake up, Mom, talk to me. Is this how you perceive your life in the retirement home? I remembered you said, Old age is not for the faint of heart. I remembered you didn't want to tell me anything more when I asked you to recall your stories.

Thinking back, I guess I never really wanted to know about the world Mom was living in all those years, especially the more recent times after Dad died: the eight years on her own in the apartment they had moved to when they sold the family house and the nine years in a retirement home daily in her wheelchair. I tried to make up for her loneliness by visiting as often as I could, but was it enough? No, probably not. Why didn't I arrange for her to move in with our family? A selfish answer. I was busy with my work, my family life, our daughters still at home, my husband traveling so much. I thought I couldn't manage with Mom at home too. I chose instead to place her in a nearby retirement home that offered excellent care.

Maybe I would not have been a good companion if I had tried to put myself in her shoes. I might have cried in despair. And that wouldn't have helped either of us. Maybe it was for my own self-protection.

I didn't want to acknowledge I was getting older too. I didn't want to know what it would be like to be old and frail. I could see what was happening to Mom, but I didn't want to ask how she was dealing with it.

Maybe there was a bit of blindness and deafness on Mom's part to the reality of old age. Maybe that was a necessary element in keeping her going day to day. Too late now, but I wished I'd asked, Mom, why didn't you tell me what it was like? Why didn't I ask you? Would it have helped? Would I have understood?

I remembered that even then as I sat beside Mom's deathbed, when there was so little time left to ask her anything, if she did wake up and talk to me, even then, I wasn't sure I wanted to ask her those questions, hear her answers, know what it was like to grow old and frail, to be so close to death. I didn't want to hear her answers.

When did death begin to creep up on Mom? I wished desperately for an answer. When did she stop doing all the familiar things she had always done, always enjoyed doing? When did that stop? One day she was writing in her journal, intelligently, keeping track of all the details of her life. And then she was not. One day she was full of stories about the events going on around her, questions about our lives. And then she was not. When did this happen? When did her connection with life stop?

I wondered, Did Mom think about this? Her own mother died when she was my age, just sixty, so she never experienced her mother getting old. I don't think she knew what it was like ahead of time. Or my Dad either. He had lost both his parents when he was quite young.

But I knew. I saw Mom almost every day for nine years when she was in the retirement home. I wished that I did not know, what I know, what I saw, what I imagine she might have been thinking and feeling. But I knew. I knew what it would be like to grow old.

Why was I obsessed with this? I thought I was empathizing with Mom, what she must have been experiencing. But no. I was seeing myself, thinking of myself. Thirty years from now. What it would be like when I was old. I always planned my life. I was always in control. I was the one who was afraid of forgetting, or choosing to forget, or no longer being able to keep track. Would it happen to me? Of course it would.

I came to know what getting old was like. I saw it happen to Mom. That's why I was so afraid. I wanted to be able to recognize the signs. I wanted to be able to plan for it. Maybe I wouldn't care then. But I sure did now.

15

Tears endless tears
Your three brothers,
Your mother and father,
Your husband, our dad,
All these loved ones
Dead.

I never saw you cry.
Did you cry
alone
silently
screaming
in the dark
night?

I never saw you cry.
Were all the tears drained
From your heart long ago?

I cry for you.
I cry for me.
Will I run out of tears
As I cry for you?

As I cried for you
In the hospital
Cancer
Shock treatments
Pneumonia
Old age

Minutes, hours pass,
Days, nights, weeks.
I'm still crying.
Will I run out of tears too?

All my tears.
My tears for you
the pain you had to bear.
My tears for me
my sorrow
losing you.

My tears of frustration
all my questions.
Would you answer?
Would your answers
comfort me now?
I do not know.

I wondered, Can I live my life better somehow, more aware, because I have seen death? What about my own mortality? Is there any way Mom's death will prepare me for my own death or for the terrible pain of losing another loved one?

I have found that going through a really bad experience is somehow less painful the first time around when you don't know what to expect. The first time I got pregnant I was so excited. My best friend was expecting a baby too—turned out she had twins. We talked about our professional goals. We'd figure out how to be mothers and career women at the same time.

Then I had an early term miscarriage and when I held the lifeless beginning of life in my hand, I was so afraid. I did not want to try again. What if it happened the second time? Mom's first child had been stillborn, the big brother I'd always wished I had.

Thankfully, I did get pregnant again. Our first daughter's birth was traumatic, emergency caesarean, and then our younger daughter a planned caesarean. How afraid I was that second time around knowing what the surgery would be like. We must have a protective mechanism that prevents us from imagining how painful these experiences might really be. I guess we might not go ahead with a lot of things in life if we knew in advance what it was going to be like.

What about death? Suffering the terrible pain of losing a loved one, does the same apply? Every time it is harder. I do not ever want to go through this again. Not that I have any choice in the matter.

When will the next time be? Will I be better prepared? Will it be me next, my death? I sometimes think that all my tears and sorrow are not really for Mom, they're for me. My own mortality. I am now the oldest in the family. In the natural scheme of things, no one stands between me and that final boundary.

Old
Older
Elder
Is that wiser?
Is that me?

Old
older
oldest
Next in line
to die
Is that me?

16

So many questions, frustrating unanswered questions. Yet somehow life continued on. My work agenda was full. I sat on three boards and chaired one of them. I had two new consulting projects to initiate, both working with not-for-profit organizations to help them establish clear strategic goals and figure out how to make progress in achieving them. Some days I wondered how I had ever managed the time to visit Mom so frequently. Most days I desperately wished I could escape for a while, to sit and converse with her, tell her what was going on in my life, complain a little, be comforted by her. I remembered that even when she could no longer understand what I was saying, she would smile her lovely smile and I reflected mine back to her.

My life outside of work was busy too. Social outings with my husband and our friends, and my brother and sister-in-law. I spoke most days with our daughters. But not very often about my grieving. I was learning to handle everyday life by keeping my deep sadness and loneliness locked inside me. I couldn't or didn't want to share my grieving. I decided, I will keep my true feelings hidden. This may not be the right approach but it's what I need to do. I'll answer, I'm fine, when anyone asks me, How are you?

This became my defence, my coping strategy, my effort to handle my deep sorrow as I believed Mom had always done. I wondered, Is this what she taught me—to push the sad thoughts away? Is this her secret? Push it down, pull it under, get it out of sight. Is this what I'm unintentionally teaching my daughters?

I didn't even tell our two daughters and my husband how hard it was for me some days to just get up in the morning, go out of the house, continue as normal, on the outside at least. How could I have done that? Not even confide in my dear family?

I questioned our daughters later, What did you think about my reluctance to speak of my mourning during those first months? Did you think me strange?

They told me, We talked about it a lot with each other. We were worried about you. We kept wondering, What should we do? But we consoled ourselves knowing that if you really needed to share your feelings you would.

If you'd asked us, we would've come home immediately to be with you, to comfort you. But you didn't. You didn't seem to want to share with us how you were feeling. We live far away. Our lives are busy. We thought you were talking with Dad and your friends. We didn't know you had decided on silence as your way of coping with your grief. And, in a way, yes, we're glad you didn't smother us with your sorrow, but we knew you knew we were always there for you.

I reasoned, This is true. I know they're right. I needed to work my way through my grieving, by myself, for myself.

I have a very close relationship with my girls. But it is quite different from the one I had with my mother. Mom depended on me and perhaps I depended on the certainty of my role as her caregiver. I didn't want to burden my daughters with my grief. They lived in distant cities. New jobs, new friendships to work out. So I chose not to share my deep sorrow with them. I knew they had loved their Oma very much and were mourning in their own way.

I remembered a scene from their childhood that was replayed many times during the five years or so that Mom's bipolar disease stabilized on the drug lithium. Calm and happy years before Mom was confined to a wheelchair after a hip replacement operation that didn't heal properly.

I remembered Mom and Dad arriving in our driveway. Dad had a "new to him" used car.

Like your new car, Dad. Looks in great shape.

Yes, he says, pleased that I've noticed. Got a good deal. Only eighty thousand miles on her and never in an accident.

Mom gets out of the car, clasping her familiar handbag, light-colored rattan, wooden handles and a brown leather strap with a clasp. She waves and smiles. She's formally dressed as always. High heels. Hair stylishly curled, newly dyed a pinkish beige color.

Hey Mom, you've got a new perm. Looks nice.

The girls rush out of the house to greet their grandparents. Our youngest just walking scrambles down the steps holding tightly to the railing. Her sister jumps the stairs in a giant leap and gets to Oma first.

I've got Oma's bag, she calls out gleefully and rushes off with the prized possession. She knows it's full of candies and she grabs the lion's share.

Oma intervenes, Come, come now. Save some for your sister. You know you have to share. And reluctantly our oldest hands over some of the loot.

During that same period when the girls were still quite young, my parents cared for our daughters at the cottage for several weeks each summer while my husband and I continued our work routine in the city and came out to the lake on weekends. After Dad died Mom became the main grandparent in their lives. My parents-in-law lived in Europe and were rarely able to come for a visit.

As young adults even after they had left home they continued to communicate with their Oma via faxes and later e-mails that I printed out and hand-delivered to her. Summer holidays and Christmas visits always brought us together celebrating as Mom loved to do.

When Mom died I asked the girls, Is there anything of your Oma's you would like to have as a keepsake? They both wanted that handbag, always well stocked with treats for the kids they were then.

I kept on with my way of coping, not speaking to anyone about my deep sorrow and loneliness. It did seem to help get me through the early days and months after Mom's death. But as time passed I began to acknowledge the truth that this strategy of keeping my grief inside—hiding it deep down out of sight, out of hearing—was not working for me. My writing had become my voice, my internal voice. I poured all my feelings into my journal. But on an emotional level I needed more.

17

I sat up in bed again in the middle of the night with the dreadful memory that kept forcing itself into my consciousness. I tried to push it away whenever it surfaced, but I could never erase it from my mind: my terrible guilt.

Always the same dream. I'm lying on the beach. My phone rings, Your Mom's been rushed to emergency. I try to get up but something's pushing me down. I try to pack my bags but nothing will fit, everything keeps falling out. I can't make it to the airport. The plane has left. My outside voice persists, You must go. My inner voice resists, There's no need to go home. Stay on. Have fun. I'm in a panic. I wake up gasping for breath.

The words of the night nurse continued to haunt me, Your mother's not sleeping. She's been waiting for you. She lies for hours looking at the ceiling, eyes wide open. I played this over in my mind. Over and over. My endless excruciating guilt. Don't worry, they said. She'll be fine. She's so strong. Resilient. I listened to them. I believed them. And when I did come it was too late.

She was on her deathbed. She had given up. She had lost heart because I wasn't there. I was always there with her—all those hospitals, psychiatric visits, doctors' offices, clinic waiting rooms. I was always there with her. And this time I was not. And she died because of that, because of me, because I wasn't there by her side. How can I reconcile this? How can I live with this guilt? No answers.

Mom died peacefully but I sacrificed my peacefulness for a long time to come. I knew Mom would have forgiven me. But I still couldn't forgive myself. I knew she needed me, me the faithful daughter always there for her. I'd failed her as she was dying.

My terrible guilt. I wanted absolution.

I came to know I was not alone with this guilt. I spoke with friends. They had their own stories to tell. It brought some comfort knowing I was not the only one berating myself. Why do we have to bear all this? All this guilt. Alone.

It was only much later that I came to understand that, perhaps, guilt deludes us into thinking we had power but didn't act on it. Perhaps guilt protects us in a way from the terrible revelation: that we had no control; that we could not have changed anything; that the situation had little to do with us; that we were in fact powerless in death, even when our nearest and dearest were concerned.

18

On Sunday morning two weeks after Easter I was sitting on our living room couch with the window open, warmed by the spring sunshine, relaxed, reading our local newspaper. I came across a poem I liked in the "Arts" section.[2]

The poet speaks of her growing awareness that her life is beginning to end as she battles cancer. She senses her death is imminent and she laments her promise to her loved ones that she would never leave them. Her final words express her acceptance of the inevitable, that she knew this day would come.

I wondered, Is the poet speaking for you too, Mom? Is this how you felt toward the end when your life was changing so much? When you could no longer hold your pen to write the loving notes you always sent? When you could no longer see to read what kept you connected with the world and animated your conversations and sustained you through so many years on your own? When you could no longer reach your wheelchair and they hoisted you in and out of bed in a sling? When you could no longer hold your fork and they asked you to eat in your room because it bothered some of them to see you struggling?

Did you know your life was ending, Mom? Did you know the day would come when you would have to leave me? You did say, I want to go home. Do nothing more. Quite clearly you said this to me. You decided the time had come.

I realized the truth that I hadn't been able to accept before. You really were ready to go. All those times you were trying to tell me, I want to go home, and I would not listen. I put my finger on your lips and said, No Mom. Not now. I need you to get through the rest of today and then tomorrow and next week. Don't go. Not yet.

I'm starting to understand better now, Mom. You chose not to leave me until our daughters were grown up enough to be here for me. You stayed until you knew they would comfort me. You decided your day had come—your birthday. I'll never have to mourn you on your death day, only on all the birthdays we can no longer share.

19

In early May about a month after Mom's birthday/death day I woke up in the night. Heart racing. Breath ragged. Flash of memory. Mom, I miss you.

In the morning, I still felt Mom's presence but I could not remember my dream. I got dressed in my black business suit and drove off to a meeting. I passed a park along the river near the rapids. I had never been there before. I felt I must stop. I looked at my watch. I was early for my appointment so I turned into the parking lot. I got out of the car and walked down to the water. Rough water rushing over jagged rocks, muddy along the shoreline. A memory came to me so intensely I could hardly breathe.

Mom takes us for a walk to the edge of a river near the rapids. There is foam on the rocky shore with frothy brown edges. My brother is in his stroller. I'm holding a doll and a little straw basket and I'm standing beside the rapids. Mom takes us there every day, in all kinds of weather. It's what I saw in my dream. Why this scene? Why now?

I had the photos that Mom had taken of my brother and me on these outings, but I had not recalled these scenes for a long time. The intensity of the memory was a physical experience that left me shaking. I went back to my car and sat there for a while until I was calm enough to continue on to my meeting.

When I returned home that afternoon, I called a close friend to tell her about my strange intense memory experience. My friend understood what I was going through because she'd been very close to her mother who died more than twenty years ago. I asked her, Was it a panic attack, too much stress, do you think?

She replied, Your Mom is with you all the time. Even though she's gone in body, her spirit is close by. You remember me telling you how I communicate with my mother. I find a quiet place. Sometimes I go outside at night and look up at the stars. I tell her what I'm doing, especially if I'm worried. I ask her for advice whenever I have a problem or a big decision to make. It helps me so much. It's the same with your Mom. She's always there for you too. Maybe that was just her way of reminding you she's nearby.

I haven't had that experience yet, I confided, that sense of comfort and closeness. I'm still troubled by Mom's death. Was that really a natural way to die? Taking away the IV so she had no liquids at all as she lay dying? Giving her all those medications to prevent pain but not enough to let her pass on? When she was lying there all those days, not eating, not drinking, not moving, did she know she was dying? Could I have done anything else to help her?

My friend consoled me, For me the deep sadness and terrible sense of loss have slipped below the surface, but I still feel so close to my mother. You'll get there too but it takes time.

133

20

Red roses
White roses
Pin one on your suit.
A red rose
Or
A white rose
Pin it on your suit.

Choose red
Joyful vibrant alive
Your mother is living.
Choose white
Pale death
Your mother has passed on.

We always got the red ones then.
Mom and Dad wore white.
Life and death
Red and white
Joy and mourning.

Mother's Day.
I must choose white.

For the first time
Today.

When I was growing up, it was traditional on Mother's Day to wear a flower corsage to church on your Sunday best dress or suit. Red or white, alive or deceased. The sign was there for all to see. Mourning was visible. Compassion and comfort were offered.

That late spring Sunday morning, my first Mother's Day after Mom's passing, I went to my closet. What should I wear? A summery dress or black? I chose black. I wondered, Will anyone notice I'm wearing a white flower on my black dress? Will anyone know why? Why is it that my mourning is invisible to most of the people around me?

A few days after Mother's Day, I attended a local art show. I was drawn to the work of an artist who depicted disease, death and rituals of mourning.[3] She had overlaid old-fashioned black Victorian lace onto detailed drawings of diseased organs taken from a period medical text. In her artist's statement she described how Victorian culture had expressed loss and grieving in an open and public way. She paralleled their mourning practices with their society's focus on making the invisible visible through advances in science, use of the microscope and new medical practices. Her phrase, "making the invisible visible," held my attention because it seemed to me that our culture today prefers me to do just the opposite—make my grief, my suffering, invisible.

I reflected, I am in mourning, yet I am expected to keep invisible what is so visible to me. No culture for mourning. No signs I can give to explain why I am sad. When someone asks me how I am and I want to burst into tears, what will they think? They don't know Mom is dead and I don't know if I should tell them.

Death. Grief. How does our society acknowledge the terrible pain I am suffering in mourning my loss? It seems to me we don't do that very well in North America. Why can't we express our grief openly? Why don't we know how to comfort? Why do we have to hide it deep inside?

21

As the weeks went by I continued to bury my pain and loneliness even deeper inside. No one seemed to want to listen. No one seemed to want to hear about my sorrow and loss. Why was that?

I questioned myself, Is this true? Is this fair? It's my fault too. I'm not trying to include anyone in my grieving. I want to work my own way through my mourning. Before Mom died, I never thought about death and sorrow, grief and loss. And I certainly didn't write about it. Now maybe I think about it too much. But that's okay. I'm sure it's normal. I also understand much better what other people are going through when they have to deal with death. When someone speaks with me about the passing of a loved one, I try to listen with all my heart and my head. Each person's experience is unique and deeply personal. And yet at some level we all say the same thing: No one wants to listen. No one wants to hear our stories. No one wants to share our sense of loss—unless perhaps they are experiencing it themselves.

I persisted in my questioning: Why are people so reluctant to respond empathetically to someone else's grief? Is it that acknowledging death makes them feel mortal and vulnerable, and that they want to push away those painful thoughts? I find it rare to be with someone to whom I can express my grief openly and spontaneously and find comfort in that sharing. When it does happen, often quite unexpectedly, I find great solace.

It happened to me the week after Mother's Day when I was working in another city for a few days. That morning in the hotel lobby I met a friend I hadn't seen for a long time. We were both rushing off to meetings but we stopped for a quick chat.

Let's get together later in the afternoon, I said. I haven't seen you in ages. So much to catch up on.

There's a coffee shop across the street, my friend pointed it out. We can meet there.

When we got together at the end of our workday, our conversation roamed easily over the details of our lives—daughters, friends, work and the recent deaths of our mothers.

My friend said, I'm writing a book. I ask everyone I know who is mourning a loved one—mothers, fathers, spouses, friends—to tell me their story. You must tell me yours and I'll include it.

That's a great idea, I responded enthusiastically. I really appreciate it when someone asks me how I'm doing and offers me words of condolence, but it happens so rarely. Why is that?

My friend replied, Everyone I've spoken with says the same thing. I think people just don't know what to say. They feel awkward.

Yes, I agreed, but why is it so difficult to say a few sincere and simple words of comfort? I saw a list the other day about what *not* to say:

She's gone to a better place.
He lived a good long life.
You must have been expecting it.

That phrase, I said, "You must have been expecting it," that's the worst I've ever had someone say to me. I don't think you ever expect death. You never plan for it. You never get emotionally ready for it. No. Death is not expected.

What a surprise it was to meet my friend there in that city a long way from where we both live. I came away comforted by sharing our stories.

A few days later my husband and I were at a dinner party hosted by our neighbor who lives across the street. I hadn't seen her for a while. We both lead busy work and family lives. She took us through the house to her spacious backyard. It was a lovely warm evening in late May. I was trying to feel relaxed. I hadn't gone out very often since Mom's passing. I kept telling myself, Don't cry. Don't get upset when someone asks you about Mom. We sat down together.

Her first question, How are you? How is your Mom? I remember you saying she wasn't well the last time we spoke.

Thank you for asking, I replied somewhat apprehensively. She died a few weeks ago on her birthday. Her ninety-fourth.

Oh, I am sorry, she responded kindly, but you must have been expecting it.

Those words made me angry. It was a thoughtless thing to say. I wanted to shout, No. I did not. I did not expect Mom to die. But, since we were friends and she was our host, I replied as calmly as I could. No. I didn't expect her to die. I truly never contemplated her dying. Thank you for asking. I continued my conversation in my head, Yes, she was old and frail and yes, her health was declining. But did I expect Mom to die? No I did not. Did I somehow mentally prepare myself for that eventuality? No I did not. Should I have? Could I have?

Visiting Mom, talking to Mom, gradually became a more and more significant part of my life as her physical and mental needs increased. The more she came to need my help and the more time and attention I gave her, the thought that she might not be there anymore simply never entered my mind.

My husband and I belong to a supper club that meets every three months at a member's house to celebrate with superb food and wine. On the last Saturday in May we sat down together and raised our glasses in a toast "to summer almost here." We were longtime friends and we were conversing comfortably at the dining table relaxing after a wonderful home-cooked meal.

I was speaking with my friend who was our host for the evening and she told me, My very best friend died recently. We knew each other for more than thirty years. She died so suddenly. I just can't believe it.

I had met her best friend only once, but we had quickly discovered we came from the same home town so we had lots of memories to share in that one brief time together. I asked, What happened? Had she been ill? How are you doing?

And my friend began to speak, at first hesitantly and then in a rush of words of pain, sadness and relief.

After a while she stopped and said, Thank you for asking. Thank you for listening. It helps so much. No one seems to want to hear.

I know.

22

The trees leafed out quickly in the warm days of early June. I usually liked that time of year, fresh beginnings, but not just then. I wasn't ready yet to experience the joy I usually felt at the arrival of spring.

I drove to the hospital for some medical tests. I hadn't been there since Mom's death. A place full of memories. I turned into the familiar parking lot. I pushed through the heavy glass entrance and walked down the main corridor past the door of the head social worker in the discharge office. I recalled her heartless words, We have to discharge your Mom today by noon. I often thought back to those last days Mom spent in the hospital. I wished I could have expressed myself more clearly to the doctors. I would have said, I needed to know the truth, the facts, the details of what was to come, of what dying and death would be like. I needed to know what palliative care meant and what I could do to help alleviate Mom's pain and my own. I needed you to communicate better with me, to have conversations with me about dying, those difficult conversations that would have helped me to make the right decisions more easily. I needed the compassionate support of the whole medical team.

Well here I was in the hospital again. But it was too late for me to say those words now. Too late for Mom and me anyway. Nevertheless I thought that what I'd wanted to say was important. I would have to find some other way to communicate that message.

I walked on past the hospital flower shop where I bought Mom the last bouquet of red tulips to celebrate her birthday morning. Across the hall was the gift shop where I hung out sometimes when I just needed to be somewhere else other than in Mom's room. I would wander around the little space aimlessly looking at what they had, reading the greeting card verses. Whose birthday is coming up? I'll be ahead of the game for once. Have the cards ready to go. It's so much nicer sending a card, receiving a card. I usually only remember at the last moment and then I have no choice but to e-mail my best wishes. I do it all the time but it never seems quite right. Happy Birthday! I'd pick up a card. Read the verse. Too sentimental. Dumb humor. I'd put it back. Something to do. One for Mom. Her birthday is coming up at the beginning of April. Now it's over and she's gone.

I passed the cafeteria where I bought all those containers of yogurt. Hopeful that, if I could just get her to swallow a few spoonfuls, she would get better. But she couldn't. I would eat the rest. I was always hungry there.

I saw a nurse walking toward me. I thought I recognized her but I wasn't sure. I didn't say hello. But really I should have. She was the one on duty at the retirement home on Mom's last night before her birthday. She had spoken kindly, Don't be

143

upset if your Mom passes on and you're not there. Some people are very private. I've wanted to tell her how much her words meant to me. I've wanted her to know Mom waited until I was there. The next morning. And I was sure she would have smiled and said, That's good. That's the best way.

I reached the end of the long corridor. I had made it. I had run the gauntlet of memories. Up one floor and there I was in the waiting room for my doctor's appointment.

The receptionist said, Take a seat. Make yourself comfortable.

Sounded as if I would be there for a while. A sign on the check-in desk read, Unattended Children Will be Given a Free Puppy and an Espresso. I couldn't resist a little smile.

I leafed through a dog-eared copy of a woman's magazine from a year ago March. Mom would have still been alive. There was an article on spring cleaning. Empty your closets, it proclaimed. Get rid of the things you've been accumulating. Make a fresh start. Should I do that? Clear away Mom's clothes and her hairbrush, her cosmetic bag, and almost full bottle of perfumed hand cream I had given her for Christmas. There were so many small familiar mementos of Mom that I just hadn't been able to throw away when my brother and I emptied her room the day after she died. We had to rush that day because the retirement home wanted us to make way for a new resident who had been on the waiting list and was anxious to move in.

Maybe it was time to do that. I would save all the albums and photos, her books and the diaries she wrote in daily until she could no longer hold a pen, or see to read, or notice what was happening around her.

23

I called a local women's shelter and asked, When is your next pickup time in our neighborhood?

It was time to deal with Mom's things. I felt strong enough to do it. I went down to the basement and found a box. I had already washed and ironed and folded the clothes I thought could be reused. I sat down beside the neat pile I had made. I held each piece on my lap for a moment before I put it in the box on the floor in front of me. Blouses and sweaters and jackets, each one had a little bit of memory tied to it. I held up one of my favorites—silky material, green and brown flowers, a small gold circle brooch still pinned on the lapel. Mom wore it last Christmas. That wasn't so long ago. I set it aside. I had to save this jacket just a little longer. I was not quite ready to give it up.

Her good shoes, never walked in as she sat in the wheelchair all those years, and her unworn slippers went into the box. That seemed easier somehow, not so connected to her. Underwear and socks, slacks and skirts, I had already discarded those. But it was the blouses and sweaters and jackets that were the hardest to let go. We selected each one of those pieces together. When she could still walk on her own, we had great fun shopping, spending hours going from store to store, trying things on, laughing when something didn't look quite right, nodding in approval when a piece worked. There, that dark chocolate nubby wool sweater and skirt with the small brass buttons. Bought on sale. A winter outfit in the summer. It was so hot in the change room. I didn't want to bother. But she insisted. She always knew exactly what would suit her and it was a real bargain. She had trouble choosing clothes for me. She would pick colors she liked. Green and brown. But blue is my favorite, especially cornflower blue, every shade of blue except hospital gown blue.

You wear too much black, she often told me. What would she say if she could see me now wearing black every day?

I picked up the white windbreaker she wore on our last picnic outing in the fall. She could still hold her own sandwich then, if I cut it up into sections, and her cup when I wrapped her hands around it and put mine over top. We were at the falls up the river. They were less torrential than they are in the spring and there was a rainbow in the light mist coming off the water.

I wanted to cry. I'd better stop now, I told myself, before I get depressed. These are just things. Mom is gone. There is no point hanging on to her old clothes. But I had to keep a few pieces with special memories attached. I would keep them in the closet of the bedroom where she slept when she came to visit. When I was missing her especially, I would hold them against my face, the fabric soft and silky or wooly and scratchy. But I would connect with her for a moment. And they still smelled of her perfume, ever so faintly.

I cleaned out a drawer I hadn't looked through in a while. At the back there was a small parcel wrapped in white tissue paper still sealed with the store's sticky label. What is it? I wondered. I tore open the paper. A bottle of Mom's favorite perfume I'd bought for her last birthday. She had worn this fragrance even as a young woman in Europe. It wasn't available here. I had brought back many bottles over the years from my earliest backpacking travels there. The excitement of watching her unwrap the little package—knowing what it was—still surprised, still delighted. I opened the bottle I'd found, the last one. The fragrance of Mom. How powerful the sense of smell, its ability to awaken memory. It too would fade.

24

This moment, this morning, first thing, it's beautiful.
Sunshine filtering through trees in full leaf. My windows wide
open. I hear the birds. I'm thinking of you, Mom. It's very
early in the morning, much earlier than I usually get up. I've
just returned from a trip overseas and my day time, night
time hours are all mixed up.

You were always such an early bird, up at dawn each day way
before us. I think you lived a secret part of your life, early in
the morning, every day. I wonder what you thought about so
early in the morning. I wonder what dark thoughts you
pondered with no one else around.

25

As spring progressed, with its longer days and warming sunshine, my deep sorrow lifted a little. I experienced roller coaster ups and downs instead of the endless black cloud of grief constantly pressing down on me. On some days I felt less depressed. But I never knew what was going to push the grief button inside me. Make the tears well up. Uncontrollable. Cause the immense sadness to surface again, the terrible sense of loss.

One particular event stood out in my memories of that spring. My daughters had just arrived home. We were going to the cottage for a week. We were out shopping for sandals and whatever else summery we might see. We were laughing, excited about our purchases.

Suddenly I saw her in the crowd. She was walking toward me. I looked away. Unconsciously, I was willing myself not to see her.

But my daughters saw her. They didn't know who she was.

Mom. Stop. This lady wants to speak with you.

Hello, I said. Good to see you again. I held out my arms. We hugged. My eyes filled with tears. So many moments, so many conversations about Mom. She was Mom's last caregiver at the retirement home. She loved Mom very much. We shared our grief for a moment.

Are you okay, Mom? Do you want to sit down? Do you want a coffee?

No. No. I'll be all right.

But for me our joyful time was broken.

26

I questioned myself, Is grief my enemy? I wear my grief like a second skin. It has become part of my demeanor. It feels embedded in my life. Will I ever be able to shed it, peel it off one day like sunburnt skin? Will I emerge one day with a new skin, a new outlook, a new perspective on life, a new future? I cannot imagine it just now.

Grief is a profound, intense and inwardly focused emotion. I'm wrestling with it. I want to banish it from my life. It's holding me back. It's preventing me from remembering Mom's life. I don't want to go on mourning her death. Mom would not want me to cry like this. I know that.

Death is what I have to come to terms with—Mom's death, Mom's life. The life before the death. That is what is important.

I have to come to terms with the idea of dying. My mortality. Perhaps, I can live my life better if I can understand death. I have to confront it and go beyond it.

I must not fear my own mortality. I must not fear death. This is what Mom wanted me to know. This is why she waited for me that morning, her birthday morning, waited for me to be there with her. To watch her slip away so peacefully. This is her final lesson. There is no fear in death.

I will understand death when I am dying and I will not be afraid.

27

I remembered a summer trip to the cottage. Where we live it gets very hot and humid in the early weeks of July and everyone goes to a cottage if they possibly can: their own, a friend's, one borrowed or rented. Everyone's in a happy mood. Escape from the city heat.

We arrived at our cottage and I was surprised by an unexpected sense of relief. I was here and Mom was not alone or lonely any more. She loved this place. Memories of her were all around me.

I'm walking in the woods. Here's the fallen log where we sat and watched the heron stalking frogs in the bullrushes. Remember. It caught one, swallowed it whole, legs hanging out its long narrow beak, one more gulp, and the frog disappeared. And then the heron sees us and takes off with a harsh, hoarse squawk, unexpected from such an elegant bird, wide wings spread, spindly legs dangling for a moment, then tucked up flat and back under the body for flight. That was the last Thanksgiving Mom was able to get to the cottage.

I'm walking in the woods to the rocky outcrop in the hot sunshine where we saw the one and only snake we ever encountered there. We were both taken by surprise. I don't know about Mom but I wanted to scream. Maybe she did too but we each needed to be brave for the other so we just stood there frozen until it slithered away. The seconds that felt like an hour, until we hugged each other in relief and started to laugh at our momentary fright. It was the smallest grass snake.

Cottage days
remind me
of you
Mom.
Fireflies in the forest
outside your window tonight.
Yellow-green, yellow-orange.
I'm trying to count them
the way we used to
sitting on the edge of your bed
here at the cottage.
This is the first night
of summer holidays
here at the cottage.
And the fireflies are out
to remind
me
of you.

There was a black and white family photo on the rough wooden walls of the main room in our cottage. Mom took it with her Kodak Brownie camera in the summer of 1954 when her parents came from Europe to visit us for six months. I recalled that all the family members I knew from my childhood were in that photo.

We're crowded together on the narrow cedar plank dock at the front of the cottage. The dock has two large iron wheels positioned halfway along its length so that Dad and my uncles can pull it up on shore in early November just before the lake freezes over.

In the back row of the photo, on the left, my father stands beside his oldest and his middle brothers, all three bare-chested, in baggy cotton boxer style bathing trunks. My Oma is in the middle—small beside Dad and his brothers. She's in a short-sleeved purple-flowered dress that she wears in several other photos I've seen of her from that long ago summer. My Opa has a bushy white beard and is formal as always in a white linen jacket. At the far right are my three aunties sitting on the dock, their legs hanging over the edge—two in sun dresses and plastic pop beads to match their outfits, and my favorite in a bathing suit that looks old-fashioned now with its short-pleated skirt and modest square-cut neckline. My brother and I are kneeling in front of everyone else, holding on to the big iron wheel on that side of the dock. I'm in my new red shorts and white sleeveless blouse with the navy and red pattern of Scottie dogs. I've turned away to talk to my brother, probably to boss him about something. I did that a lot. I was the older sister after all. My three white bathing capped cousins are sitting in the water in front of the dock.

In my memories that was such a happy summer before Mom's deep sadness when her father, my Opa, and then her mother, my Oma, died; before her battles with cancer and bipolar disease; and long before her frailty, and blindness, and death.

Why was it every time I had a positive memory I was pulled back down by a negative one? The endless roller coaster of emotions was exhausting.

But for most of my time at the cottage that summer I'd felt relaxed. Some days I realized with surprise, I had gone for hours, walking in the sunshine, playing in the water, without thinking about Mom. Was that bad? I reminded myself how important it was to celebrate life as Mom had been so good at doing with her decorated cakes and homemade cards for every possible calendar event. Other days I had a big ball of sadness inside me that came to the surface and wouldn't go away.

My best friend came to the cottage for a few days in mid-July. I hadn't seen her in a while. She's tall and blond like me. We met ten years ago in an open market in New Delhi of all places. I think we were attracted to each other partly because we've always felt a bit awkward about being so tall.

She brought me a photo she took last Christmas when we went together to visit Mom at the retirement home. There we were, Mom and I, looking at each other and laughing, Mom very much alive in that photo. I realized with a shock that the image of Mom I'd been carrying in my mind was the dying Mom, thin white hair pulled back from her forehead, eyes closed, wrinkles smoothed away, the open O of her mouth, breath sometimes harsh and rattling, sometimes so soft it was hardly present.

The dying Mom, that was how I was remembering her. But in the photo my friend brought me Mom was vibrant and joyful. That was the image I needed to replace the death mask etched in my memory since Mom's passing.

Tears were streaming down my face. I had forgotten this Mom. I'd been trapped by my overwhelming grief and my anger and frustration at how things worked out at the hospital, at how death happened. I'd forgotten the real living Mom. Now perhaps I could begin to turn the clock back to the times we had shared, both happy and sad, as life is.

Evening set in and it grew cool by the lake. My friend and I were sitting in the main room of our cottage beside the fire my husband had just lit and the flames caught at the birch bark we used to get it started.

My friend said, Tell me about your Mom.

Where should I start? I replied.

At the beginning, she suggested.

That might take a while. I'll read you a story from my journal instead. One of the stories about Mom's life that I wrote down a few months before she died. I used to read them to her over and over and we would laugh together as we shared her memories. Here's one of her favorites and I began to read.

Mom's Story: Meeting Your Dad for Coffee

Here comes Sunny with her big book under her arm, the soldiers call out teasing me as I step into the canteen to meet Claude, your future Dad.

The big book is my dictionary—a Dutch to English dictionary. World War Two is over. May 1945. I've just met your father. His battalion is based in Soest just outside The Hague where I live. I learned English in school but I'm a bit rusty, so I carry my dictionary with me so I can speak correctly.

It's spring but still cold. I'm wearing my warmest outfit. The only one I have. It's made of men's suit fabric. Nothing else was available during the war. I had to trade a good part of my carefully hoarded black market supply of soap, nylons and chocolate to get the fabric and have the suit made. And to get those things from the black market I had to trade my beautiful heavy gold bracelet that had been an heirloom gift from my mother. But you can't eat gold. It's not a useful trading item with the farmers when I go to buy some meat and vegetables to feed myself and the old couple that the army has billeted in my home. In the last months of the war the dykes along the sea were bombed and the low-lying farmers' fields were flooded. They lost everything and were lucky to escape with their lives.

The black marketers knew where to sell my gold bracelet so it brought me a good supply of items that the farmers' wives wanted. The suit is very warm and I wear it every day. It's the only one I have but I think it becomes me.

I look around the soldiers' canteen. It's dark and smoky inside but I see him over there toward the back of the room sitting alone at a table with a coffee cup and a cigarette. He's waiting for me. Real coffee. I can smell it. I've been drinking dried chicory leaves since my supply of coffee ran out quite a while ago. I take a sip from his cup and a drag from his cigarette. Such treats!

28

After the Labor Day long weekend in early September we continued to enjoy summery weather. I was home again after the peaceful cottage days I spent with my husband and best friend. I woke up one morning so lonesome. My first thought was, My child is dead. No, it's Mom. She had called me Mom so often—to the point of being absurd sometimes—when she would call out at the retirement home, I want my Mom. And someone would call me in a panic and I would drop everything and go to explain it was me she wanted.

Funny sort of. I had to make light of it. Otherwise I would weep which I did often enough the last few months when Mom would lament, I'm too old to live anymore. I want to go home. And I would say, No, don't go. I need you, Mom. You're the one I tell my problems to. I know you don't hear me anymore. You don't really understand, but it helps me to describe what's bothering me, just to say it out loud. I love you so much. Don't go. Stay with me.

That September morning I was so lonesome. I remembered my painful sobbing when Mom left me the first time. I was four. She had to go the hospital early to give birth to my brother.

Caesarean. That's how I'd been born as well. Mom and Dad took me to my aunt's cottage for a week ahead of time. They kissed me good-bye.

Dad said, I'll come for you in a week. By then you'll have a new brother or sister.

I hope it's a sister, Dad. Can you make sure of that?

The week went by so slowly. Every day I asked my aunt, When is Daddy coming to get me? I liked her very much and it was fun swimming and going out in the boat fishing with my uncle, but I felt so left alone. At the end of the longest week ever, Dad came to pick me up. Fireflies, some flashing green, others yellow, lit our way up the cottage lane to his old 1950s car. A magical ride. Windows rolled down, warm summer evening breeze, crickets chirping. I had him all to myself that short ride. Just Dad and me. Me sitting in the front in Mom's seat.

We walked quickly down the long hospital corridor. Is it a girl? I asked excited. Jumping up and down.

Wait and see, Dad smiled.

We walked into Mom's room. She looked so tired. She held out the baby for me to see.

Here he is, your new baby brother.

Fifty-six years ago.

She'd left me so many times—so many hospitals, cancer clinics, psychiatric wards. So many visits. After school. Evenings on my own.

Now she'd left me forever and I was so lonesome sometimes.

I was also relieved. That was a hard thing to say. It felt wrong but it was true. When I woke up, my first thoughts were always, how is everyone? Each of my loved ones. Is there anything I can do to help? And there was Mom, still on my mental list. But I didn't have to worry anymore about how she was doing, what would happen to her next. When my cell phone rang I knew it wouldn't be the retirement home calling for me to come at once.

29

It's Thanksgiving
and I'm sitting here
on the old log,
the fallen tree trunk
at the edge of the forest
beside the lake
not far from the cottage
where we sat the last time
you were here.

A long time ago
when you could still walk
the rugged path through the pine trees
to the water's edge.

Today is bright and the sky is that blue
it only gets in October, deep cornflower,
like the linen dress you made me
A long time ago.

The day I'm remembering was soft gray overcast.
We sat on this log and watched a heron land,
its wings lifted for a moment

like an archangel's
high over its silver gray back
before folding them in repose
and landing
soundlessly.
A long time ago.

Despite the warm sun
there's a north wind today
turning up the edges of the water lily leaves.
Shiny green in the sunlight.
Deeply veined underneath.

I am at peace
being here
remembering you.

There were still leaves on many of the trees and bushes that
mid-October. Bright red, gold, and orange-brown. The days
were sunny and warm for the season. My brother and I were
at the cottage together with our families for Thanksgiving. It
was more than six months since Mom's passing. All our kids—
our two girls, my brother's two boys—came home to celebrate
with us, our family tradition. I cooked the turkey and
vegetables and made cranberry sauce, dressing and gravy. My
sister-in-law brought a pie. After dinner we stood around a big
bonfire on the beach talking and laughing. Part of our
tradition too as long as no strong wind was blowing. During
the day we collected fallen branches and dragged them over to
the fire site. Housecleaning the forest was how I always
thought of our annual activity.

There was something I needed to ask my brother. I'm sorry to be talking about Mom's passing in the midst of our holiday get-together, I said, but I find it so hard some days to live with the sadness and sense of loss. How are you dealing with this?

He answered, hesitantly, I guess I'm slowly getting used to it. But I still find myself some days in front of Mom's retirement home. I've driven up the street and there I am without even thinking about it.

Yes, I do that too sometimes. But how do you feel day to day? I persisted. I wanted to know I wasn't the only one feeling sad and lonely and missing Mom in the midst of this happy get-together. Maybe I was beginning to realize I needed someone to talk to about my deep sorrow.

Well, I try to keep busy, he replied. But I think about Mom all the time. I'll never get over her not being here with us. It took me months to live through Sunday afternoons. I would suddenly feel guilty that I was not visiting Mom. And then I didn't know what else I should do that afternoon. What about you?

I'm journaling as always, I told him. It brings me some comfort to write about my memories of Mom and how I'm feeling. I try to keep up our family traditions. I'm not much of a cook but I did find that preparing the Thanksgiving meal was somehow cathartic—not exactly fun—but creative in its own way, reenacting what Mom used to do.

Yes, I'm sure that helps you, he continued. I need something different to do just for myself. Perhaps I'll learn to play the piano again just as Mom did. I think you're trying something new as well. You're blogging about your thoughts and feelings on mourning Mom in a coherent way to a broader audience. When I read what you've been writing I see we have very different memories of her. I didn't realize all you went through. I would have to say that I don't really remember when Mom was told she had cancer and later bipolar disease and you went to visit her all those times in the psychiatric hospital. I guess I was just the little brother, not paying much attention to what was going on around me. I went off to university and then worked all those years in the bush as a surveyor. I was out of touch with our family for long periods of time. Now we're each trying in our own way to find solace and move on.

Yes, that's true. Thanks for telling me this. I hugged him. It helps a lot to know I'm not alone with this immense weight of sadness and loss. That it's okay. That you feel this way too. That we can share our memories.

I'd never considered this difference in my brother's relationship with Mom, that he hadn't experienced Mom's illnesses and the loss of her presence at home as I had.

Our Thanksgiving Day conversation cheered me up as did having our daughters at home to celebrate all together at the cottage.

During the summer months I'd started to feel my grieving was less intense. But as autumn set in and the days grew shorter I was feeling deeply sad again. I was beginning to realize I really did need help to work through my mourning. I needed someone to talk to, to ask me, How are you? I needed to know that I could answer that simple question frankly and openly. I was not coping as well as I should be, I thought. I was too sad too often.

30

A week or so after Thanksgiving I decided it was time to sort through some more of Mom's things, which I had carefully stowed away in our basement. I'd taken care of the clothes a few months ago. But I'd not yet looked at what was in the white plastic storage box of albums, loose photos in envelopes, folders of kids' art, and other papers Mom had collected over the years. I thought it would give me some comfort to look at the photos, in particular. The photos Mom had taken of happy outings when my brother and I were growing up and also the older photos from Mom's family that reminded me of the stories she had told me of her brothers and her parents.

At the bottom of the box I found a scrapbook I'd forgotten about. Bright, flowered plastic cover, so different from the faded brown leather photo albums I'd just been looking through. I recalled that I'd bought it for Mom when she first moved into the retirement home for the celebratory photos we took when we visited her and the ones I sent when we were on holidays. Travel stories and messages our daughters had e-mailed her were glued in. And some poems I'd written. One was about me as a kid. I smiled remembering the moment.

Claudia Chowaniec

I'm seven walking with
Mom
arm in arm to the cemetery.
All Saints and All Souls
to visit the graves of
her parents
in the town she called home
here in the old country.
Mom wearing black. Mourning.
Me
excited to be up this late.
Candles flickering on gray stone.
Cold November night. Solemn.
My grandparents.
I do remember.
Long ago.
They came to visit once.
Oma thin hair pulled back
in a bun nape of her neck
silk dress deep purple
small pale flowers
white lace collar cuffs
gold rimmed glasses.
Opa tickling white beard and black suit
always white shirt and tie formal.
Gone. In the grave. In the cemetery.
All Saints and All Souls
Mom is crying.
I try to remember

My Oma and Opa.
It's hard so long ago.
I was three when I last saw them.
Now I'm seven.

When I gave Mom a copy of this poem I taped an old photo to the top of the page. A photo Mom had taken. Me standing in front of my grandparents' grave. My hands folded prayer-like under my chin, looking down. Solemn. On my best behavior. I remembered looking down, admiring my brand-new black patent shoes. When I told Mom what I had been thinking about that moment so long ago, we laughed together.

31

I've always found November hard to adjust to. But that first
November after Mom's passing was especially difficult. The
shorter days, frequently gray, below zero temperatures,
flowers dying, leaves blowing off the trees and bushes.
Through the summer and early autumn I was often sad and
sometimes quite lonesome. But generally I was coping fairly
well I thought. I was getting on day to day—going to work,
engaging in my volunteer activities, maintaining our familiar
family and household routines. Summer warmth and
sunshine. Cottage memories of happy times together. Not
every day a dull routine of waking, working and sleeping.
Remembering Mom every moment.

After I returned from the cottage I started going to the gym
on a regular schedule and signed up for a series of sessions
with a personal trainer. Steps I thought proved I was
returning to normal again. But as November unfolded
confidence in my ability to handle my grief waned and I
slipped back into the deep sadness I had experienced in the
very early months after Mom's passing. Was this a relapse?
Was that possible? I'd been making good progress I thought.

I got a call from my closest cousin. Mom was her godmother. She was about my age and we used to see each other frequently when we were growing up, but we'd lost touch over the years. She told me her mother, one of my favorite aunts, had passed away. She was a few years younger than Mom and they had been great friends. Her parents had come from Europe as well. Mom had felt she could confide in my aunt about how difficult it was to be so distant from her homeland and my aunt understood from her own parents' experiences. It was a bond they shared, knowing what it was like to be an outsider trying to be accepted in our small town where everyone was related or knew everyone else through a family or friend connection.

Dad's two brothers and two sisters were very welcoming. But Mom had found it hard to adapt at times. They frequently kidded her in a friendly way when she didn't understand their jokes. Mom had asked one of her sisters-in-law how to clean something that really needed scrubbing and my aunt had teasingly replied, Soap and water and elbow grease. Mom had apparently asked, What is elbow grease? That was a classic tale that was still being told when I was old enough to hear about it.

My cousin and I had not seen each other or spoken together for quite a while, but we talked on as if we called every day. We talked about how we were both the oldest in our families now and how that made us conscious of our own mortality for the first time, the reality of our aging, a sudden unexpected confrontation with the possibility of our own death.

My cousin said, You know, there's hardly any of our family left to ask about the way things used to be. I miss hearing their stories so much.

She told me about deaths in the family and funerals she had recently attended, just as my aunt used to do when our families got together after not seeing each other for a while. She spoke of people I hardly recalled because I had been away from my home town for years.

My cousin told me about her mother-in-law who passed away a few months ago at age ninety-eight. The elderly lady had proclaimed, I'm going to live as long as the Queen Mother. She hadn't quite made it but what a feisty person she'd been. On her ninety-seventh she had ordered fish and chips and a beer for her birthday lunch at a local restaurant. She hadn't eaten much of her food or finished her pint, but she loved being taken out by her family. She only spent a day or two at the hospital before she died.

My cousin went on to tell me about two sisters who died recently at ages ninety-five and ninety-six. She said, They were the daughters of the woman who rented some rooms to your Mom and Dad when your Dad first came back from the war and your Mom arrived on the ship carrying the war brides from Holland. One of my aunts was in love with the man who later married the older of the two sisters. They went out together for quite a while and then he broke it off. He was the love of her life. The man she eventually married was her second choice. She committed suicide in mid-life. Did you know that? We often said, She always seemed so sad. Was that why?

All this talk of death. I don't want to hear about all these deaths now, I said crossly to myself, even though I was really pleased to have reconnected with my cousin. But for my aunt and my cousin these were the conversations of the day to day in our small town—births and deaths. I just didn't like to share in that chat about people dying. Not long ago I had overheard some friends at a dinner party exchanging news on recent deaths and I had shivered inside to think I knew of death too but didn't want to talk about it.

Why is that? I thought. I'm completely contradicting myself. Through all my time of mourning I've been complaining that there's no public conversation about death, and here I am, guilty of that very problem. Why don't I want to hear about the deaths of others? Why don't I want to talk about Mom's death?

I knew some of the answers. I was concerned about getting depressed. I worried that people would break down in tears as they told me of their loss and I would have to comfort them just when I was feeling vulnerable and selfishly wanted to be comforted myself.

When Mom was in good health she was the one who made sure we stayed in touch with the growing families of Dad's brothers and sisters. When each of them passed on it was always Mom whom the cousins called first. Mom was the messenger to the rest of the family to let them know what had happened. That November day my cousin called me about her mother's death and now it was my role to pass on the news, just as Mom would have done.

32

Minutes and hours pass
then weeks and months.
Clocks confuse, distort,
fail to mark the passing
time stands still.
Minutes hours days
Time races on.
Calendars, too, confuse distort.
Force me into others' celebrations:
All your birthdays, Valentine's,
St. Patrick's, Easter, Mother's Day,
Dinner parties, summer holidays,
Thanksgiving. Now Remembrance Day.
How did I get to here?

Growing up, Remembrance Day, the celebration on November 11 for all the war veterans, including the living, was very important to our family. Weeks ahead my brother and I looked out for the familiar red velvet plastic-backed poppies. We would drop a dime or a quarter into the donation box, pick out a poppy and pin it on our coat. Relatives had served on both sides of the conflict during World War Two and Mom insisted we remember each of them. The weather was invariably gray, raw and frequently rainy. From my earliest memories, Mom, my brother, and I walked to the war memorial in the central square of our small town. A Highland band played and I ran along the street beside them, marching and dancing to the pipe and drum music.

Before we left home Mom would remind us to pray especially for her brothers, the uncles we had never known, who had been killed in action in Europe during World War Two. We always promised solemnly that we would. But it was hard thinking about someone we didn't know, trying to imagine what they would have been like.

They were so young, Mom said. And that was how I pictured them. Always young, smiling, handsome in their uniforms in the photos by her bed.

Dad was at work unless November 11 fell on a weekend. They had two minutes of silence on the factory floor, but he rarely came with us to our town's memorial service. Perhaps his own war memories were still too close.

One scene from my childhood was particularly vivid. Shortly before Remembrance Day, ten years after arriving in this country, Mom had been sworn in as a citizen by the justice of the peace, the man who ran the pharmacy on the corner of King and Courthouse not far from the war memorial on the square. It was a strange moment: solemn in that familiar, everyday place, Mom standing behind the wooden counter with the druggist holding the Bible. Mom serious and proud. Dad, my brother and me.

But this Remembrance Day, the first after Mom's passing, was remarkable in its own way—sunny and warm and so calm not a leaf was moving. Not many were left on the trees, but a few remained on the red burning bushes in the front garden. I called my daughters in the morning. I wanted to share my thoughts with them before I set out alone for the memorial service held in the center of our city at the grand carved stone and bronze statue honoring the valor of our soldiers in three wars.

My dearest daughters, I want to remember with you all of our family members who served in three wars: Grant, Dad's oldest brother, in World War One; Dad and cousin Doug; Mom's three brothers who did not return; your father's grandfather, Karol; and great Uncle John; your father's parents, Zygmunt, Krystyna, and her mother, Maria, in World War Two; Robert and Allan, sons of Grant, in the Korean War.

Remembering all of them. Remembering to remember.

The day after Remembrance Day, November 12, turned out to be a difficult one for me. I couldn't get out of bed. I cried all day. I knew they would come, all the memories from the past. But why now? Mom died seven months ago. When was I ever going to get over this?

I called my brother. I'm so upset. I don't know what to do. I'm so terribly sad and I'm worried about being depressed.

That doesn't sound like you, he reassured me, in bed for the day. But it's okay. Memories of our family's wartime experiences make me emotional too. Maybe it's because we grew up listening to all their stories. Our parents wanted us to remember what happened on both sides and now they're gone, even Mom.

I feel guilty about this, staying in bed, crying all day, I said. How can I be so weak? And, you know, at the same time, I think, why should I be ashamed of crying? My deep sorrow has been reawakened by the emotions associated with Remembrance Day, this public celebration of war and death. Our culture acknowledges that so why shouldn't I be allowed the space for my mourning?

There seemed to be levels of grief so distinct I could mark them on a measuring stick of mourning. Some days my sense of loss was so intense it weighed me down like a heavy rock pressing on my chest and it was only with an enormous mental push that I could heave myself out of bed. On the day after Remembrance Day I could not. An extreme point on that measure of grief and loss.

Two days after Remembrance Day, I felt different again. I could record my pain and loneliness in my journal. The previous day I had not even been able to put my feelings into words. I wrote that I was comforted a bit by the realization that there were peaks and valleys in my grieving. Not every day would be as difficult as the day had been just after November 11.

I went for a long walk. I saw a late-blooming dandelion in the hoar-frost whitened grass. Then another and another. I remembered being a kid again running home excited clutching the first dandelions I had found. Mom, these are for you, I called out as I ran into the house. Already wilted, she had put them in a vase and set them on the table. They're so beautiful, she said, smiling at my excitement.

And there I was that recent November day bending down to pick the dandelions, tears running down my cheeks. So out of season—dandelions in November. There just for me.

I walked on, a small grove of trees, bare branches, black silhouettes in the low afternoon light. A few gnarled old pines. Someone had gathered the small tight cones and piled them around each trunk to make it easy for the squirrels to find them in the snow. Each tree had a plaque: Norway Maple, Black Pine, donated in loving memory. I would do that in the spring, a tree in honor of Mom. She would have liked that. She had planted a tree for each of her four grandchildren at the cottage.

Remembering to remember. I knew there would continue to be levels to my grief. Sometimes intense. Yes. But also joy sometimes in the memories with the tears.

33

It was now more than seven months since Mom had died. Yet I persisted in asking myself, Why do I find it so hard to talk to people about my mourning? I'm usually candid and articulate about what's on my mind. I write about my deep sadness in my journal. I blog about grieving the loss of Mom. Is part of the problem that our culture expects us to be upbeat all the time? When was the last time I tried to honestly answer the simple greeting, How are you?

I recalled I had responded openly to that question recently with unhappy results. I was at our community center a few blocks from home volunteering at a pre-Christmas fundraising event and a neighbor asked, How are you? I haven't seen you for a while.

Well, I replied hesitantly, my Mom died in the spring and to be honest, I still miss her most days. Especially now as we're getting closer to Christmas, I'm so sad sometimes I don't want to leave the house, so I'm really glad to be here today helping out.

Oh, that's too bad, my neighbor replied and she turned away, abruptly I thought, to talk to someone else. Had I been too candid? Not the expected or accepted response? I was hurt but

I had to consider the situation. Had I blurted out my emotions and she hadn't known how to respond empathetically? I had come to realize a lot of people weren't comfortable talking about death and grief. No wonder I was so reluctant to speak with anyone about how I felt.

I'd been burying my sadness for a long time, even before Mom's death. I had worried about her health. I had been helpless to help as she became more frail. I had feared her dying. I had feared losing her. All these feelings had been with me for a long time and I'd been pushing them down deep inside me, hidden out of sight. I had to in order to live my life, work, look out for the others in my family.

I reflected. Most of us have less experience with the dying and death of loved ones today. We often move away from our family and the friends we grew up with. We rarely live anymore with aging loved ones. We are not close by to see them faltering as they age and move toward death and to prepare ourselves for their passing on.

My father died of a heart attack seventeen years ago. It was early March. We had been together for Christmas and I had driven my parents back home. We talked on the phone once a week more or less. I remembered distinctly the last time I spoke with Dad. We joked about something silly and we laughed and laughed. Dad was a rather somber man so the lightheartedness of that conversation stayed with me. And then my brother called to say Dad was dead. Just like that.

My parents-in-law who lived overseas also died suddenly a year apart. My husband and I were not there with either of them when it happened. We arrived on each occasion for the funeral and burial and then we flew home again.

I made it through the dark autumn days of November. I realized my grief would always be with me. Sometimes crushingly intense, sometimes tinged with happier memories of what Mom and I shared. I would have to learn to live with that.

But I also realized I had hit a wall. I couldn't continue locking everything up inside me. I didn't want to anymore. I decided to phone my neighbor whose mother had died a few months before Mom.

She answered and I said, I've been wanting to tell you this. Mom died in the spring on her birthday. I thought I should tell you. She was surprised. I'm so sorry, she said. I didn't know. I remember you often spoke of her, when you moved her to the retirement home, when she had to be in a wheelchair, when you were looking to buy a sling to move her in and out of bed. You mentioned she hadn't been well but I didn't know she'd passed on.

I asked her, Do you think we could have coffee together? I would really like to speak with you about all this.

Yes, she replied, of course. I understand what you're going through. Thank you by the way for your kind sympathy note when my mother died. I should have spoken to you sooner but I haven't seen you out walking as you used to do.

We arranged to meet a few days later at our local coffee shop. It was a dreary end of November day. No snow yet. I stepped into the warm buzz of conversations in the cafe. There were Christmas decorations in the windows and a special holiday coffee with a peppermint stir stick advertised on a poster over the counter. My neighbor was waiting at a table in a quieter corner.

I asked what she would like to drink and put in our order for coffee. I sat down beside her. Tell me, she said gently.

And out it poured, my story. All my sorrow and all my tears.

We talked for quite a while. What I find most difficult to accept, she said, is that I can never be a child again, not in any way. My mother is gone. I am alone now.

It's strange you say that, I responded. I feel I've lost my child. I was Mom's Mom for so long. I've lost my sense of identity. I can no longer be a daughter without a mother. My caregiving role is gone.

Yes, it's hard to figure out who we are now, she replied. But you know what's helping me move on? Grief counseling. I go every two weeks to our local hospice where my mother spent the last painful weeks of her life. I tell my counselor how I'm feeling. It's really helping me a lot. Why don't you give them a call?

I don't know if I'm ready to speak to a stranger, I said, but I'll think about it. Thank you for listening and for your advice.

I was quite sure the old saying "time heals" would be true in time. But it was difficult to believe it right at that moment when I was feeling such emptiness inside. I could say to myself, I am working through my grieving and it is hard work, and I hope that in time I will come to a more peaceful place in remembering Mom. Making progress.

Part 3

Journey toward Renewal

34

It was the evening of December 5, just before St. Nicholas Day, the Dutch celebration Mom introduced into our family's Christmas traditions. St. Nicholas brings gifts for the good kids and coal, or whatever's the modern equivalent, for the wicked, if the current parenting rules allow for these distinctions. On that evening each year when our daughters were young, we would put out cookies and milk for Santa and the elves and carrots with green tops for the reindeer. In the morning we would discover everything had been eaten and small presents and candy left behind.

I decided I would start with the Christmas ornaments. I'd taken down last year's tree in a hurry and the boxes were in a jumble. I emptied one out. At the bottom was a small brown envelope addressed to our daughters. A note from Mom dated five years ago. Handwriting shaky, even then, barely legible, but filled with love in her own words.

Keep the coffee hot. I might drop in, she had written. Here's five dollars. Buy your Mom some flowers. Say it's from her Mom. She loves flowers as much as I do and you know she brings me a bouquet whenever she can.

I thought back to that time. She was already in her wheelchair, helpless to go anywhere on her own. Always hopeful.

I finished arranging the decorations. Cleaning the silver was next on my list. I collected the pieces I would need for the parties and dinners I usually organized. I remembered thinking, It's a bit early, I know, but I like that looking-forward time. Anticipating family gatherings. Waiting for our daughters to come home. Visiting with friends and neighbors. Reflecting on past Christmases.

I sat down at the dining room table. I picked up a teaspoon, one of a dozen in a cornflower blue velvet-lined box. I haven't used these in years. Oma sent them for me when I was born and Mom had them engraved with my initials. I rubbed away the tarnish until it shone and put it down on the cloth in front of me. I unwrapped other pieces of silverware marked with the initials of relatives whose names I couldn't recall, family members on my mother's side I never knew. Each one given as a gift, perhaps saved from destruction, carried to safety, hidden away during World War One or Two. Serving spoons, a cake knife, flatware. Mom had given them to me over the years, for Christmas, birthdays, my wedding. Silver spoons with crests from cities and countries I brought back for her from my own travel adventures. Now all these familiar mementos were here in my possession.

I stopped. I held my head in my hands. I was overwhelmed by memories of what Mom and I always did together during this festive season. How could there be a Christmas without her? How would I get through these celebratory days?

I'd never really considered asking for professional help in dealing with my grief. But in that moment I finally acknowledged I needed help.

35

The next morning I called our local hospice. It was in an old stone house a few blocks away. I'd been there a few times for the annual Hike for the Hospice fundraiser.

Do you offer grief counseling? I asked. I'm not sure I'm eligible for any of your services because Mom was never a resident. But I have a reference from my doctor who thinks I would benefit from professional help.

The receptionist answered, Yes. That's fine. We have a group session coming up on Getting through Your First Christmas without Your Loved One.

Well, that's certainly right on topic I thought. But I hesitated. You don't offer one-on-one counseling?

Not at this time. Perhaps early in the new year. Would you like to attend this session?

I guess so I replied somewhat reluctantly. How will I be able to express my emotions in a roomful of people? How will I bear their immense sorrow at losing their own loved ones? I will probably end up crying for them and for me.

The phone rang early in the morning on the day the session was scheduled. It had been snowing hard since the previous night, an enormous storm, the first of the season. I'm calling from the hospice. I'm sorry but we're canceling because of the weather. I was so relieved.

But, a few days later, the counseling program called back to say they were rescheduling for the following week. Do you plan to attend?

Yes. I guess so.

On the evening of the session I drove to the hospice. I found a parking spot on the street a few blocks away and walked slowly through the snow still wondering if this was the right thing to do. The hospice looked cheerful. There was a brightly lit Christmas tree in the curve of the driveway and an evergreen wreath on the front door. I opened it and stepped into the friendly warmth.

A volunteer greeted me, Hello and welcome. Have some tea and cookies before you go into the meeting room.

A circle of comfortable chairs and sofas. A fire blazing at the far end. Quiet conversations. I sat in a large plaid armchair close to the door in case I had to escape. The counselor came in. She was young. She told us her name and began to speak firmly but gently. She used the word *bereaved* frequently. Another word I was not accustomed to speaking, as it had been with palliative, when they said it at the hospital, We're discharging your mother. She now needs palliative care. I knew the meaning but I hadn't thought of it in reference to myself.

193

Bereaved.
I am bereaved.
I am bereft.
I am dispossessed of a life, of hope.
I am deprived of a relationship, of Mom.
My bereavement.

The counselor asked us to introduce ourselves and tell why we had come. There were eight of us. A boy and girl and their father. An older man. A middle-aged woman and her mother. A young woman. And me.

I said, I'm here because my mother died and I've been mourning her for eight long months. I have this big ball of grief inside me and it's hard to live with. Christmas is looming and I need help to get through this celebration.

I don't remember what the others said but they had their own sad stories. All our loved ones. All our losses revealed.

The counselor told us, Many things will have to change now. It will be difficult. You will have to decide how to make Christmas easier on yourself. You will have to choose what you can do and what you cannot do. You must not be concerned about others' expectations. You will have to consider how you want to honor the person who is gone. How to include the memory of that person in your own celebrations and with your families and friends. Protect yourself. Put yourself first.

I considered this idea. It was a new perspective for me. It forced me to think outside myself. That was not easy. As a mom and as a daughter until recently I'd been in the habit of thinking more about everyone else.

She continued, Only do what you think you can handle. Make it your Christmas with the emotional strength you have now, at this moment. Start new Christmas traditions.

I resisted that idea. I wanted to shout, No. Everything must be exactly as it was when Mom was with us for Christmas. But then I realized, Maybe that was no longer possible.

Many things will have to change now, she went on with her lecture. What things? I thought. How will I know what to do and what not to do? How will I deal with this?

Avoid the triggers, she said. That makes sense, I agreed to myself, but how? Everything about Christmas makes me think of Mom.

Only do what you can handle or you might lose it. Make Christmas easier on yourself. Give yourself the freedom to say yes or no. Do what you can. Don't be concerned about others' expectations.

But who will decorate the tree? Who will prepare the Christmas Eve meal? The Christmas Day dinner? Who will greet the well-wishers who come to our home?

I'd already done those things for years on my own, but I always had Mom's presence to support me. Now I felt confused and frightened. I would have to take on the whole responsibility myself for ensuring our family traditions continued on.

I'd felt Mom's loss especially at Thanksgiving. Still I did get through with my family's help. But I feared Christmas would be much more difficult. There were so many traditions interwoven in our celebrations. Christmas Eve was when we opened most of our presents together in the candle light around the tree with my brother and his family. Afterwards we went to a late church service. When we returned home we ate a meatless meal of Polish dishes my husband prepared. The next day we hosted Christmas dinner with other family members and a few friends who had no family close by. On Boxing Day we organized an open house for our neighbors. It suddenly seemed too complicated. I didn't want to take on all those activities. I was afraid I might cry too frequently, feel depressed, and spoil this joyful season for everyone around me.

36

The evening before Christmas Eve I was sitting alone by our lit-up tree. Our daughters had finished decorating it when I got too teary eyed and had to stop and disappear for a while. I was remembering all the trees Mom and I had decorated together. Here in this house. Thirty-five trees. After we were married, Mom and Dad and my brother and his family came to our house to celebrate every year and, later, Mom on her own in her wheelchair transported here from the retirement home.

Thirty-five Christmas trees we shared together, Mom and I. That was a lot of trees to enjoy. I wished there'd been one more.

My youngest came to sit beside me. Do you remember the lovely photo your friend took last Christmas? I asked. We were sitting by the fireplace in the retirement home living room, our hands resting on Mom's. Three generations linked together. Our hands intertwined. For the last time. That was the last time you saw your Oma, I reminded her.

The last time I saw Mom truly alive was in her room by the window as I was leaving for my holidays. I turned and waved, See you soon.

She went so suddenly, from her wheelchair, to the hospital room, to her grave.

I know I've mentioned this before, I said to my daughter. Mom put great value on the importance of being an interconnected link in a family chain. She often spoke of the role of daughters in passing on traditions from one generation to the next. I'm feeling so troubled. Mom is gone and I can't consider myself a daughter any more. That role is over. It's up to you and your sister now to help me carry on our family's Christmas traditions.

On Boxing Day, instead of hosting our usual house party, we decided to keep it simple and just invite my brother and his family for brunch. It was a bright blue winter day, a dusting of snow on the ground. No major snowfalls were predicted that might delay our daughters' flights back home later in the afternoon to celebrate the rest of the season with their own friends.

After our meal we were sitting around the dining room table talking about favorite gifts, my sister-in-law's excellent Christmas cake, plans for New Year's parties.

Those eggs benedict you made, my brother said, were really good.

That's a rare compliment, I countered.

I didn't know you could cook that well, he teased me back.

I'll tell you my secret for the hollandaise. I used packaged sauce but added real butter and cream so it tastes homemade.

You know, I reflected, I feel tranquil for the first time in a long time. I made it through Christmas. I'm grateful for your support and for the memories we shared and all the joyful times over the holidays. I turned to my husband, Thank you for preparing the fish dishes for our Christmas Eve meal and for suggesting we just do a simple brunch today.

My dear daughters, I'm so glad you could both be home this Christmas. Thank you for helping me decorate the tree and cleaning up after all our get-togethers. You're always fighting even at your age. You must have conspired together to be on your best behavior.

No, Mom. We're more grown-up now, Mom. Maybe you haven't noticed. Maybe other Christmases you were really weighed down taking care of so many things, especially making sure Oma felt included in our celebrations. You seem more fully present now than ever before.

I guess that's good, I replied. I don't have as many things to think about. How will I get Mom here? Can we make it up the back steps? I hope your cousins come on time to help lift the wheelchair. Should I feed Mom at the table, with us, or beforehand? How would that make her feel watching us eat? None of this to worry about. That is a big change.

My brother and sister-in-law and my nephews, thank you for hosting Christmas dinner when you realized I didn't feel up to doing it this year and for helping me in the noisy crowd of our family celebrations to forget my sadness for a while.

Later on, when we had cleared away the dishes, said good-bye to my brother and his family, and driven our daughters to the airport, the house seemed very quiet after all the festivities. I went to my office to e-mail my friend. My dear, you're grieving yourself for the loss of your loved one. And yet you faithfully wrote me today with your determined message when I complained about being tired out by all the Christmas events. Pick yourself up, girl, and get on with life, you told me. That's what your Mom would want you to do.

I silently thanked my family and friends. You encouraged me out of the darkness of my deep grief and into the light of your love, faith and hope for the year ahead. I'm sure I will slip back into sadness and loneliness sometimes. But I am assured now that I can pull myself out again and again.

37

Very slowly like a tightly closed springtime leaf I started to open up a bit at a time. The November conversation with my neighbor about the deaths of our mothers was an important first step. I didn't realize at the time what a breakthrough that was. My reluctant decision to attend the grief counseling session took me another step forward, even though I could hardly bear to speak of why I was there or listen to all the painful stories of others' suffering.

Christmas was over and the New Year would soon begin. After dropping off my daughters at the airport mid-afternoon I walked through new-fallen snow to the park where the last dandelions in the hoar-frost-whitened grass had marked that recent difficult Remembrance Day. The plaques on the trees for loved ones. The hoards of pine cones for winter hungry squirrels and field mice.

I returned home, took down the Christmas tree and tissue wrapped the precious decorations from Mom: horse hair stars, silver gray, golden blond, from her grandfather's team; glass balls; paper cutout snowflakes; a porcelain angel with gold foil wings. All the memories of past Christmases washed over me but with less sadness than before.

Time to begin the New Year. Time to make a new start. Time to create new traditions. We all say it.

I've never really considered January 1 the start of a new year. For me it's always been the beginning of September. From school days I suppose. Weather cooling. Activities changing. But this year I'm grateful for the idea of the New Year. Turn the page. Turn over a new leaf. Time to change my outlook on Mom's death. Time to remember what Mom gave me in life, not what she took away in death.

38

The day after New Year's the hospice called, We have a counselor available who can meet with you on an individual basis. Are you ready for that?

Yes, I said. Yes, without hesitation.

The first appointment was for the second week of January, Thursday at 10:30, for one hour with a different counselor at the same hospice where I had gone for the group session before Christmas.

I drove around the curved driveway past the front door and the big Christmas tree into the parking lot. Most of the spaces were reserved for volunteers. They must have quite a few, I thought, because all were taken. I parked out on the street a block away. I climbed over a large snowbank and onto the sidewalk. I trudged slowly back to the hospice lodged in an attractive old Tudor-style home. A simple modern two-storey residence had been built onto the back of the building.

I was apprehensive but grateful it was a clear blue winter day, cold, calm and sunny. Dark days made me gloomy. Tentatively I pushed open the front door and stepped into the welcoming warmth I recalled from my first visit.

The receptionist greeted me and pointed to the coatrack and the blue paper slippers. I cringed. Those institutional blue slippers reminded me of the blue hospital gowns Mom wore when they took away her clothes at the psychiatric hospital, the blue gowns of her last days at the retirement home. I hated that color of blue.

I'll call your counselor and let her know you're here. Please have a seat there by the door where you can see what's happening in our living room. Thursday is a busy day for outpatient programs.

I sat down, nervous, as if I were meeting my teacher on the first day of school. Would I like my counselor? Would I be able to speak candidly with her? Would she listen empathetically? I recalled the young woman who had led the group session before Christmas. I was quite certain I wouldn't be able to open up to her.

And there she was, my new counselor, walking briskly down the hall toward me. A warm smile, tall, athletic build, slim trousers, a fleece vest, sport shoes, mid-sixties, short gray hair, stylish glasses.

Welcome to our hospice. Let's get a coffee. They've just set out some homemade chocolate chip muffins for the volunteers and the people who come in for the day program.

I liked her immediately. I was sure I would be able to speak openly with her. She would help me.

Let me take you on a tour of the hospice, my counselor said.

This is the living room where residents meet with family and friends. Individuals under our care who are still mobile and able to live at home also come here for various activities. The library is just around that corner. It's well-stocked with books, pamphlets and tapes. You're welcome to use it whenever you like. Here's our dining room. Between meals we use it for arts and crafts and playing board games. The coffee pot is over here and the muffins. Help yourself.

She continued down the hall with me following behind, clutching my mug of coffee and half a blueberry muffin wrapped in a paper napkin. I was glad she was taking the time to orient me. I expected I would be coming here for a while. She pointed to a small enclosed outdoor garden.

In the spring this space is filled with snowdrops and crocuses and then daffodils and tulips. You'll see, she promised me. I helped to plant them. Here's my office. This is where we'll meet every two weeks at first and then we'll see how you're getting on.

She closed the door behind us. Quiet at last. Finally on our own. So many people out there: staff, volunteers and residents. So much to take in, to become familiar with.

The room was painted soft peach with well-worn but comfortable brown leatherette armchairs and a shelf packed with books, file boxes and pamphlets. Sit wherever you like, she gestured.

I considered. I think by the window overlooking the snow-covered lawn and down to the frozen river. There was a flower vase on the round table between us. And a box of tissues. I sat up straight, uncomfortable. Was she expecting me to start telling her why I'm here?

Let me tell you a bit about myself, she began.

That's a relief, I thought. I don't have to jump in at the deep end. She's going first.

I started out as a nurse on the cancer ward in our local children's hospital, she told me. Then, I got a degree in social work with a specialization in palliative care and counseling. I've been here at the hospice for almost seven years. We'll figure out a schedule for our meetings. What about you? Whatever you feel comfortable telling me. We'll have time to get to know each other.

I replied, hesitantly, I'm not used to talking about my grieving. It's been nine long months since my mother died. In November I came to realize I desperately needed to seek professional counseling to express what I was feeling and get it out in the open.

You might like to know, she said, that many people don't come for grief counseling until a few months after the death of their loved one. We find most people need some time before they are able to articulate what they're feeling and be open to our suggestions for what might help.

I didn't know that. I thought I was strange not wanting to talk to anyone about my grief.

No, not at all.

I've also worried about my inability to get back to normal—whatever that means.

I think that everything you do when you're mourning is normal, she replied, normal for you. There are some general patterns of thinking and feeling that most people tend to experience over time at different stages of their mourning. We'll talk about that in more detail, but as long as you're not suffering extreme depression, whatever you're going through is your own way of grieving. Don't be afraid of that.

I don't think I'm experiencing extreme depression. My mother had bipolar disease so I know what that can be like.

I was getting tired talking about all this stressful stuff. My seat felt hard. It reminded me of the gray leatherette chair I sat in for so many hours pulled up close to Mom's bed, waiting for her to wake up and speak to me.

My counselor must have noticed my discomfort. She stood up and pulled some material from a file on her bookshelf. I'll go over these pages with you. They describe a number of ways that people express their grief and we can explore how relevant they are to you. This will give you a benchmark you can use to compare with your own outlook.

She's making me feel I'm doing okay, I thought, relieved. I told her, It helps me to know I'm not alone in my reactions even when they seem extreme some days. Nights when I can't sleep, overwhelmed by loneliness. Mornings so depressed I have trouble getting out of bed. Days when I can't concentrate on my work.

Okay, that's it for today, she said, and graciously wrapped up our conversation. You can take a copy of these pages I reviewed with you and we'll talk more about them next time. See you in two weeks. She looked at her schedule. Is this a good day for you? A good time?

I took out my agenda book. I like to plan. Get it down in my calendar. Something I can control. Yes, it works for me. Thank you.

39

My second counseling session was in the fourth week of January on Thursday at 10:30 again for an hour. Another calm and sunny winter day. Still lots of snow on the ground. Much easier the second time. I had no trouble finding a parking space. I walked with more enthusiasm along the sidewalk to the front door of the hospice. I greeted the receptionist. Hung up my coat. Left my boots on the mat by the coatrack. I ignored my distaste for the blue disposable slippers. I'd brought my own this time and sat down to wait for my counselor.

When I saw her coming I jumped up and walked down the corridor to greet her. Already a familiar routine. Coffee and cookies. Her office. My seat by the window again. A small bouquet of pink tulips on the round coffee table.

Your flowers are lovely, I commented after our welcoming hug.

Visitors bring them in for their loved ones and share them with us. So how are you today? Tell me how you spent the last two weeks.

I stiffened. Felt anxious. I became apprehensive now when anyone asked that simple question, How are you? I'd gotten into the habit of avoiding a direct answer. I wanted to say, I don't know. I don't like talking about myself. When I looked at her, unanswering, she said so genuinely, Tell me how you're doing.

I struggled to be honest. The time seemed to pass quickly since our first session. That's a good sign. Usually it creeps by. How have I spent my time? I work full-time. I volunteer in the community. My days are very full or they used to be when I had Mom. I would stop in to see her whenever I had a spare hour or so. She was so close by. It was no hardship. But now I have time to spare. It still seems strange. I used to collapse into bed at night, relieved to have gotten through another day. Now it's quite the opposite. I find myself staring into space sometimes, almost unconscious of where I am or what I'm doing. I have trouble concentrating. I even go to bed sometimes in the middle of the day. I can't believe it, but I do.

What about your husband? What's his response to your mourning?

He understands I have to go through this, but he can't really share my mourning. He was not close to his parents. I asked him once, Do you miss your mother and father? He said, Not so much my mom. She was a shy quiet person. We didn't have any point of contact. Nothing to talk about. But hardly a day goes by when I don't think of my father. We didn't see eye to eye on very much so I don't miss his presence or having conversations with him or anything specific like that. But I wish I'd tried harder to understand him. I'm sorry we weren't closer.

That's a very candid answer. What was your response?

His answer surprised me. We'd never spoken of this before. It made me realize again that it's my own fault if I feel no one understands what I'm going through. I don't make enough of an effort to explain my feelings even to my husband. We often walk out to our local pub at the end of our workday before dinner for a pint or two to talk over the day's events and what's coming up. I'm certain he would listen patiently to anything I had to say about being sad and lonesome missing Mom. But I don't bring it up. I've just chosen not to. Not his fault.

Do you have children? I imagine they're grown-up.

Yes. Two girls. They're both away but we speak almost daily. We're fortunate to have e-mail and Skype and cheap long distance rates. I remember what a big deal it was and how expensive to call Europe when my grandparents were still alive. My mother would book the call in advance, usually on Sunday when it was cheaper, but also much busier. We would hang around waiting for the operator to put our call through. Sounds like ancient history to our kids. Mid-1950s. When we were finally connected, we would stand beside the phone mounted on the kitchen wall and take turns asking the same questions, giving the same responses. But it was wonderful to hear my grandparents' voices.

How are your daughters dealing with the death of their grandmother?

I twisted self-consciously in my chair distressed by that question. I replied with some hesitation, I don't really know, I have to admit. For some reason I don't quite understand myself, I don't speak with them about my grief and I don't

211

tend to ask them how they're mourning Mom's passing. That must sound strange when I tell you how close we are and that we talk so frequently. They loved their Oma immensely and faxed and then e-mailed her regularly and had great visits with her whenever they came home. They spent weeks at the cottage with my Mom and Dad when they were young so they were always very close to their grandparents. I know they miss her but they have their own busy lives.

Your questions make me feel I've failed at being a good communicator, especially with my daughters, I told my counselor. I know I should be talking to them more about how I'm feeling and then I'm sure they would confide in me about their own grieving.

There's no reason you should feel guilty, my counselor reassured me. Over the next few months I'm sure you'll become more open about expressing your feelings and ready to talk about how you're doing. You've gotten used to hiding everything inside, pushing your emotions down out of sight.

I wish I'd asked Mom how she dealt with her mother's death, I continued. And also my father's. She suffered in silence. Maybe that's the approach I learned from her. Keep your thoughts and feelings to yourself and just get on with life. Not a helpful model. I'm recognizing that. I need to reach out to my daughters and talk to them about mourning Mom or I risk passing on to them Mom's way of handling her sorrow. Knowing how she had coped might have helped me now. Mom eventually got severely depressed and was diagnosed with bipolar disease when I was sixteen.

That must have been hard on you.

Yes, I became Mom's caregiver at an early age. I know it's awful to say, but there were times I deeply resented this, especially when I was a teenager. I couldn't talk to her about anything that was troubling me. I felt she wasn't there for me when I needed her. I sometimes wonder if that's why I feel so guilty about not having been there for her when she was dying. Guilty that I resented her being sick so often when I was young. My feelings get so mixed up sometimes.

Tell me more about this guilt you're feeling about her death.

I'll try but this is hard for me. I was away on holidays when Mom was taken to the hospital. I didn't come home right away when my brother and husband told me and when I did come she was already in a coma. I never got to say good-bye.

My counselor consoled me, I can understand why you're still troubled by this.

I took a deep breath. I had said it. I had admitted my guilt. I was relieved she didn't try to offer some psychological explanation for why I hadn't returned home sooner. She simply acknowledged how full of remorse and guilt I felt. I reflected, Maybe my counselor's approach is to help me pull to the surface the memories that are troubling me the most, all the thoughts I have kept hidden for so long.

She continued, Perhaps it would help you to know that a single episode of food inhalation into the lungs rarely results in pneumonia. It usually takes a number of incidents over a period of time until the body is weakened to the point it can't expel the food any longer and infection sets in. It could have happened at any time. You should not feel so much guilt about not being present at that moment.

I was grateful for her comment. I wanted absolution. I wanted an excuse. At the same time, I was shocked to realize that in truth I had had no power to alter the course of events. Even if I had been there the whole time I would have been powerless to keep Mom from dying.

My counselor continued, You mentioned earlier that you have spare time now in your daily schedule. What are you doing differently?

I'm writing, I told her. Trying to write. In my journal. Every day. About Mom. Her dying. My grieving. What I'm feeling. What my life is like without her.

When did you start?

A year ago Christmas. The retirement home gave Mom a pocket-sized journal. I remember thinking this is a bit thoughtless. She can't write anymore. But I consoled myself knowing they gave all the residents the same gift. The previous year it had been a pen in a wooden box. I started to write down everything Mom said in that little book. She wasn't speaking much anymore so everything she said suddenly seemed very precious.

I also wrote down all the stories Mom had told me. I would say, Mom, tell me about your brothers always getting into trouble, about moving to Holland before the war and designing jewelery in the silversmith atelier and weaving tapestries, and meeting Dad after the war and the fun you had together going for drives in the army jeep on the hard-packed dunes of the sea coast near The Hague. Tell me your stories again. That was the beginning of my writing.

When she was in the hospital, I wrote about my frustration with the members of the medical team who didn't give me any direct answers when I asked, How is Mom doing? Will she get better? I think they knew she was going to die. I don't know why they didn't tell me. It might have helped me prepare for her passing.

After she died I continued journaling about my mourning her. What I wrote flowed out of the depths of my pain and loss. I miss her so much. And I regret so many missed opportunities to ask her what she thought about dying and the afterlife.

You're still writing now? my grief counselor asked.

Yes, I have to. I keep her memory alive by writing about her every day. She seems very close when I wake up in the night and recall some detail of our time together and I get up and scribble it down on the notepad I keep by my bed. I am amazed at how many memories do come back: events, experiences, conversations that I didn't even realize I remembered. She always said it's important to remember to remember. I think it brought her great solace when she was grieving the loss of her three brothers and her parents to remember them consciously, to tell us about them and to celebrate their memories and all their birthdays, long after they had passed on—a special cake for each of them and later for my Dad as well.

She's somehow back with me when I'm writing. She's sharing this time with me. She encouraged me to write more but I was always too busy. Whenever I did write something about the history of the area where our cottage is located, my travel adventures, and the ups and downs of parenting, I would read her my stories. She was a good critic—make your characters come alive, help them tell their story, add more detail. That's good. Work on it some more.

I believe she would approve of what I'm trying to do. Help others who are suffering the loss of a loved one to find some comfort in my sharing what I'm going through. Help give expression to their personal experiences through my describing what I'm feeling, especially the awful guilt of not having done enough. I'm coming to realize more and more that if we're able to seek solace from those around us we'll feel much less alone. Here I am blurting out nonstop. What was your question? What got me started writing? Why am I writing?

I hope what I said made sense. You pushed a release button inside me with your questions. I often don't really know what I'm thinking or feeling until I say it. And it's only by saying it out loud that I can begin to understand Mom's dying and come to terms with my grief. I need your questions to help me express my thoughts and feelings. They've been buried deep for so long.

My counselor wrapped up our session. We'll keep this appointment time—Thursdays at 10:30—if that suits you? When you come again it will be February 14. Why don't you bring me something you've written that reminds you of how you and your Mom celebrated Valentine's Day?

Sort of like show and tell at school, I said, teasing my counselor a bit. I liked the way she was gently pulling out the stuff inside me that had been hurting for so long.

40

I was feeling a slow sea change inside me after the first two sessions with my grief counselor. I was amazed what a relief it was to talk with someone who asked me questions about myself and truly wanted to hear my answers.

I recalled the conversation I had last spring with my best friend after my panic attack and my strangely powerful memory of Mom, my brother and me at the rapids on the river near our home. My friend had told me that I should try to live more fully in the present, in the now, if I wanted to find peace. Talking out my feelings was helping me to do that. Live in the present. Move beyond my endless grieving.

It was a warm day in early March and I was in my car with the windows down on my way to lunch at a favorite Italian restaurant with a friend I hadn't seen since Mom died. I had the car radio on and a professor was speaking about *post traumatic growth*. It caught my attention. I was familiar with *post traumatic stress disorder*, which may affect men and women who have lived through the terrible experiences of war. But the idea that a traumatic event in our lives, such as the death of a loved one, could result in growth was new to me. I considered the concept appealing: that on my grief journey I might develop a deeper awareness of the world around me and that greater self-reflection might lead to personal growth. I thought I should explore this idea. It may also help me understand how Mom was able to survive so many traumas in her life and ultimately come to a peaceful place within herself.

I'd always been inclined to look for rational answers to what was troubling me. Putting a name on my tumultuous thoughts and feelings would help me as I tried to make sense of what I was experiencing. I decided to do some research on post traumatic growth and see what I could learn.

41

Two weeks later I was back at the hospice for my next session. My counselor told me, We've been celebrating Valentine's here for the past week so we can include all the members of our day program. How are you doing? Did you bring me some of your writing? Would you like to tell me more about your mother?

I miss Mom very much. I was Mom's Mom, her caregiver most of my life so in a way it's like losing my child. I have a lot of regrets. I never brought her home to live with our family. I could have been with her more of the time. I could have done more to make up for all the losses she suffered, all the pain she had to endure. I sometimes ask myself, Is this what my mourning is all about? Suffering for my own guilt? A private selfish experience of loss? Going through unending days of sadness at the loss of Mom, when it's really remorse for what I didn't do? I wanted her blessing, her forgiveness for all my shortcomings.

I continued, I've also felt the fear of death. Her dying. My mortality. My own death in time. I've come to realize consciously for the first time that I too will die. Perhaps that's the hardest of all to accept and come to terms with. I don't know. There's so much I don't understand.

Does it help you to speak of all this?

Yes, very much. I've never thought about any of this before. Mortality. My own death. At least not consciously. Maybe, it's that my thinking only becomes clear to me when I say it out loud. Thank you for that. I appreciate your asking, your wanting to listen.

You asked me to bring you something about how we celebrated Valentine's. Here's a poem I wrote last week and a card Mom made for a dear friend a long time ago. I'll read you my poem.

My lover sends me
tulips
on Valentine's
two bundles bright
flaming red
always the same
one for me
one for you
Mom
two bundles, two vases
yours and mine
shared between us
better to give than receive
you always said
two bundles, one vase
too many
flaming red tulips
too many in my vase.

I've also brought a beautiful Mom-made Valentine's card to show you: shiny red heart-shaped cardboard with delicate white lace glued around the edges. Inside there's a verse addressed to Mom's best friend of fifty some years. I have this memento because Mom's friend sent it to me when she was downsizing her house to move into a retirement residence.

She wrote, This is so precious to me. I couldn't throw it out when I was sorting through the few things I will have room for in my new place. I don't have your mother's address in the retirement home. Please take it to her with all my love and fondest memories of our long friendship. I wish we could see each other again but I don't expect that will be possible.

I told my counselor the story about how this dear lady attempted to teach my mother to drive fifty years ago. Mom's friend has driven her out to a country road and she stops the car to let Mom take the wheel. Mom is feeling quite confident. She's figured out how to change gears. She drives down a steep hill and the car is picking up speed. Mom yells out, How do I stop the car? Help. How do I make it stop? Mom's friend had forgotten to tell her where the brake was. It's so obvious, she later said to Mom, I don't know how you couldn't find it.

I thought that story was really quite funny. Mom's friend had been my Brownie leader and I recalled her somewhat impatient and meticulous nature. She was rather embarrassed that she'd failed to point out the brake to Mom. They never tried the lessons again and Mom never learned to drive.

42

My fourth counseling session was coming up and I was reflecting on how they were helping me. When my counselor asked, How are you? I answered truthfully. I found it a relief to talk about my long hidden thoughts and feelings. I was growing conscious of a need to externalize my feelings and to share them with others who were going through similar experiences mourning the loss of their loved one.

I called a longtime friend whose father died two or three months before Mom. We set a date for me to come out for a visit. When her father passed away we talked on the phone about his last months and how she was doing. But I didn't go to see her which I know I should have. I had known her father quite well from the time twenty-five years ago when he came with his new wife to our home where we were hosting the wedding reception of his daughter, my friend. She hadn't wanted to go back to her home town to get married because none of her friends were there anymore and she was not fond of her stepmother.

I wasn't able to say the right words then to comfort her in losing her father because I didn't know what it was like. Mom was still with me and I never contemplated her passing on. And my father died so suddenly. I never had to be his caregiver. He was there alive and strong and then he was gone.

I reassured myself, I'll be more compassionate and consoling now. I'll be able to speak with her about mourning Mom. She loved my mother very much and we can share so many memories.

I drove out into the country where my friend lives in a lovely restored log home. It was a mild late February day and the sun was shining warmly. She came outside to greet me and we hugged tightly. It had been so long since we'd seen each other. She had been ill when Mom died and her husband had come on his own to the funeral. We had so much to catch up on. We went inside to her living room and sat down in the comfortable quilt-covered armchairs she pulled up close to the cozy log fire burning in the large gray fieldstone fireplace. An old-fashioned fancy china teapot and delicate rosebud-patterned cups were set out on a table beside us—and my favorite—homemade brownies.

How have you been? I couldn't wait to hear her stories.

My neighbors out here in our small community have been so supportive, she told me. You know dad died almost a year ago. I can hardly bear the thought of the first anniversary of his death coming up so soon. Shortly after his passing one of my neighbors called to say she would like to visit me to express her condolences. I didn't know her except to say hello so I was surprised she wanted to call. Well, you won't believe what she brought me. I was so touched. Wait a moment and I'll get it to show you.

Here it is. She held out a pale pink delicately knitted oblong quilt made up of many small woolen sections. I took it in my hands and held its softness against my cheek.

It's a prayer shawl. My neighbor explained that, as the shawl was being knitted square by square, the ladies at her church prayed for me and for my dad as they worked together. They hoped it would be a source of comfort for me when I wrapped it around my shoulders. That it would soothe my grief when I felt its warmth around me. They also wrote a poem about my dad and pinned it to the shawl.

What a wonderful old-fashioned gesture that your neighbors out here in the country still practice, I said. You're fortunate to have such thoughtful and caring people around you to share your grief and receive their condolences. I wish someone had offered me such consolation. None of my neighbors acknowledged Mom's death with a visit or sent over food and condolences.

My friend acknowledged, That's true. They have helped comfort me. But I cannot forget those last six weeks when my brother and I took dad to the seniors' home. His sad, sad eyes when I left. I know he willed himself to die. He'd been a strong, proud man. He didn't want to be there in that home. He felt he had lost all dignity. That was the hardest part—no dignity. I didn't have power of attorney, my stepmom did, and she didn't want to deal with him at home any more. I would've liked to bring dad to our house but my stepmom wouldn't agree to that either. I had no control. That was what was so hard when I had spent so much effort to help make the last years of his life better. You remember I always invited him and his wife to spend holidays with us and I made the long drive to visit as often as I could.

I nodded empathetically. I knew how gracious and hospitable my friend always was. Such a thoughtful and loving caregiver. She would have done anything to make her father's life easier, more comfortable. And then to know in the end that she had no power to do anything to help him, to prevent his wife from putting him in the nursing home, that must have been unbearable.

What could I do? She held up her hands in anguish. What else could I have done? You know one of the hardest things for me now that dad is gone is seeing the clouds. Almost every day. Dad was fascinated by them. When I was a little girl we loved to sit beside each other for hours and look at the clouds and laugh together at all the funny shapes we could discover. As dad's Alzheimer's advanced his visions of cloud formations became even more fantastical. We sat beside each other for hours and looked at the clouds. But their shapes changed. They became evil and frightening. Now the clouds are there to remind me of him. Almost every day.

But let me tell you one of the good things I've experienced. My brother and sister-in-law and my husband and I got together two weekends ago. For the first time in thirty-eight years, that was when dad remarried, we got together, put our feet up and relaxed. We sat out on the front porch in the almost spring warmth and I realized how long it had been since we were together just enjoying each other's company and laughing. Not thinking about the old folks. Not second guessing what our stepmother would be up to next to make our dad's life harder. A tremendous relief at one level. Not to say I don't miss him terribly.

I told my dear friend how hard it's been for me since Mom died and how going to my grief counselor these last two months is helping me speak about my deep sorrow and that I finally feel it lift a little.

I'm sorry I wasn't able to come to your Mom's funeral, she apologized. I loved her so much. But I was sick after dad died, heart-sick for a long time. I didn't go out of the house for weeks last spring. Thanks for sending me a copy of the eulogy your brother wrote. I learned many things about her that I hadn't known. I remember you telling me about her dealing with cancer and bipolar disease. But I didn't know she had been married and lost her first husband and her three brothers in the war. She suffered many hardships but she never let it show. I remember how gracious and kind she was, a real lady.

My friend and I drank tea and ate her delicious brownies and we shared more stories about our beloved parents. We comforted each other sharing our memories.

A few days after I went to visit my friend, a neighbor I hardly know stopped me as I was walking down our street. After he had expressed his condolences, he said the most unexpected thing, Now you're an orphan. That's how I think of myself, an orphan, since my mother and father died. He continued, Every day I wear something that belonged to my father. Whether it's a jacket or a tie or his watch, I feel he's still with me. For the last twenty years it's my daily ritual.

We hugged awkwardly and went on our way, but I was comforted. We each find our own way to hold on to the memory of our loved one.

I continued to be surprised sometimes by what people said when they did take the time to speak with me and acknowledge Mom's passing. I considered what my neighbor had expressed. He spoke of us being orphans now that both our parents are dead. That's true, but it's not how I think of it. For me losing Mom is about not being a daughter anymore. My loss of a role. Who am I now? I need to find new meaning in my life. I have to let go of what I've lost. A daughter no more.

We each had our own story to tell. For me sharing these experiences of loss was helping me feel I was not alone with my grief. And I began to hope that in time there would be more happiness and joy in my memories and less of the endless sadness and that awful sense of guilt.

The passing of my friend's father and my neighbor's mother were the first of many deaths that had occurred during recent months. The husbands of two school friends died in March. A drinking buddy my age, who we used to hang out with at our local pub, died of a heart attack on his way home from a holiday cruise. The husband of a colleague who grew the most beautiful flowers died. The mother of our youngest daughter's school friend died.

I was entering a new stage in my life when my peers and I—friends, neighbors and colleagues—had to learn for the first time for most of us how to bear grief, how to express it, how to share it, how to somehow find solace, and move beyond it. I was coming to understand that the secret is we're not alone with our grief and sense of loss, if we choose to reach out. I was beginning to realize that we each experience loss in our own unique way. I was finding consolation in speaking with others and trying to put into words what I was feeling. I was feeling less alone.

43

It was the first day of spring, twelve days before Mom's birthday. The first anniversary of her passing. Last year, I was so heartbroken I couldn't bear to think of ever celebrating again.

Mom has just died.
How can that be?
Her birth day.
Her death day.

Dying on your birthday.
What did you think?
That we would forget you,
That we needed
a special day
to remember
you?

How could you
die on this day
of celebration and music?
Your music, your piano,
still here in this room
where you left us.

Violin cello bass
Your three brothers.
You on piano
All dead.

I do not need to mark today
The day you died.
It is your birthday.
It will always be your birthday.
Birth day
Death day.

The day you died.
It is your birthday.
I cannot celebrate
The day you died.

I mourn.
In time
I hope
I can celebrate.

44

I invited my brother and his wife for brunch on Mom's birthday. It was Good Friday. The day on which she was born. Strange coincidence. My brother said he'd come but his wife was at her sister's.

I greeted him, Come on through the house. We're sitting outside on the terrace for the first time this year. Keep your jacket on. It may be cool.

How have you been? I asked. I haven't seen either of you since the new year. Thanks for the Valentine card. As you said in your note, Valentine's always reminds us of Mom and how enthusiastically she celebrated the day.

Have you taken up the piano again? I continued. Or your guitar? You mentioned you were going to take lessons. Do something for yourself. I've been seeing a grief counselor every two weeks. She's very good at getting me to tell her how I'm feeling. Do you think that would be something you'd like to try? I could ask her for an appointment for you.

No thanks. That's just not me. I couldn't imagine spouting all my thoughts to someone else. I'm doing fine. I have a new real estate project I'm working on and it's keeping me busy. Keeps me from getting weighed down by my feelings. But I'm glad to hear it's helping you.

I'm serving eggs benedict again. Remember, you actually told me you thought they were really good when we had brunch together at Christmas. So what do you think? Do I get another compliment?

When I was thinking about Mom's birthday coming up I wasn't sure what to do. Should we celebrate? Should I make a cake to remember her? It was what Mom would have done. Well, I did bake a cake so we can celebrate.

That's great. You know I have a sweet tooth. Besides you do bake quite well.

Well that's a record—two compliments in one day, I teased my brother.

45

Easter morning,
celebrating again.

Setting the table
family breakfast
remembering Mom
all our celebrations
spring birthdays
hers and mine
Valentine's
St. Patrick's
Easter.

I open a drawer
looking for paper napkins
Easter eggs colored birds
bright bunnies tulips lilies
one or two the same
a few left in a package
remnants from all
the Easter morning
special breakfasts

shared with Mom
all those years.

I spread them
haphazard
on my table
overlapping
like a crazy quilt.

Easter morning
celebrating again.

46

I started my first blog: www.GriefShared.com. I thought that telling my stories about grieving the loss of Mom might help others find comfort in sharing what they were going through. I wrote every few days. I described what I was doing, how I was feeling, how I was getting through all the celebratory days on the calendar when I didn't feel like joining in but didn't want to spoil the event for my family.

I received responses from readers who wrote to tell me how much they valued what I was saying. All my correspondents have been women. I wondered, Do men choose not to read blogs about grieving or do they just not want to express their feelings on-line?

I've been quite astounded by how many of the comments said almost exactly what I was expressing. Reading them made me realize how universal people's response was to grief. Yet I really didn't know that until I put my stories out there and started hearing what others were experiencing.

What a beautiful read, one woman e-mailed me. Thanks so much for sharing. When my mother died I just wasn't prepared. I take some comfort in knowing the last time I saw her we hugged and as always I said I love you. A day doesn't go by that I don't think of her. I could never imagine a day without her in my thoughts.

Another woman said, It takes courage to share grief publicly. My dad passed away in 2001 at the age of sixty-three from a massive heart attack. Almost ten years later I still can't mention or think of him without an urge to cry. I still celebrate his birthday.

Even people who haven't yet experienced the loss of a loved one said my stories reminded them to be conscious of expressing their love to the living. An artist friend remarked, Reading your poems and texts has caused me to reflect on the delight that my own mother is and how lucky I am to have her in my life.

These exchanges with readers really encouraged me to keep writing the blog even though I found it hard some days to put my feelings out there in such a public way.

47

I was sitting with my grief counselor in the hospice garden on the faded white-painted wooden lawn chairs. The air was fragrant with lilac, lily of the valley and honeysuckle. Late April, getting close to my birthday at the end of the month. This was our sixth session.

How are you? she asked, her usual welcoming question.

I responded hesitantly. I always try to answer your simple question honestly. Let me tell you something funny. My older daughter e-mailed me the other day and asked, Do you ever lie a little to your counselor?

I wrote back, It's a good question. I do find it difficult some days to articulate my thoughts and feelings. Sometimes I go early to my counseling session and I sit in my car thinking about how to answer that simple but demanding question, How are you? At first I would ask myself, Does my counselor really want to know?

But I trust you and I know you expect me to answer honestly. Otherwise there wouldn't be any point in my being here. But I do have to think through what I want to say. I often make notes ahead of time. It's still hard for me to put into words what I'm feeling.

I understand, she said. Tell me right now. What are you thinking?

Just about this moment, how beautiful and still it is.

Being in the present?

Yes. I'm able to do that better now. I was always dashing around from one place to another, one activity to another, planning what I needed to do next with half my mind, listening to Mom with the other. Why is that? Is that normal?

Everything is normal when you're grieving, except perhaps extreme psychotic reactions. You're doing it in your own way, in your own time. It's your grief, your journey and the path you're on keeps changing. That's what's surprising you, even troubling you, isn't it?

Yes.

There are many case studies of individuals who have gone through a deep personal trauma—a terrible crisis—who have survived and moved on to reach a new stage. It's different for everyone. You are continuing on your path to a new place in your life, new feelings, new thinking and new actions.

But how will I get there?

You will have to find your own way. But I will be here to help you, she reassured me. We can talk about it whenever you like.

I told her I'm experiencing a strange new sense of loss that's quite different from what I've been feeling all these months since Mom's death. There is an emptiness inside me, as if I'm missing something. It's hard to describe because it doesn't make sense.

She explained, Perhaps you're feeling this way because the intensity of your grief is subsiding. This sense of emptiness—could it be that the deep and all-pervading grief is starting to lessen?

This can't be normal, I said. How can I be sad about losing the pain of my grief? Why should this make me feel empty, as if something I've hung on to for a long time is slipping away? This should be a good thing. But it's uncomfortable. I'm experiencing a space inside me, an emotional gap that makes me feel empty somehow.

To my immense relief, she said, that's all right. That's normal too. It's as if you've had an enormous ball of grief inside you for so long and now it's starting to shrink a bit. So there's some space there.

How do I fill that space?

How do you want to fill that space? That is the question you have to answer for yourself. But I will be here to help you.

My grief counselor and I decided I would start coming once a month, instead of every two weeks. She thought I was making good progress expressing myself more openly. I agreed. I was feeling much less depressed than when I began seeing her four months ago.

As we were saying our good-byes, she reminded me of the Hike for the Hospice fundraising event in two weeks' time.

I hope you'll be on my team. All staff members here compete in a friendly way to see which team can raise the most money. It's our tenth anniversary this year and it's always been a sunny day.

I promised I would come. I told her I'd joined the hike a few times in the past never thinking how important this hospice would come to be in my life.

48

It was my birthday, the end of April, exactly four weeks after Mom's. A milestone. My sixtieth. The beginning of a new year and a new decade.

Me at 60
Mourning Mom.
Mourning being 60.
Mourning how much my life has changed.

I asked Mom once at New Year's what her resolutions were for the year ahead. She answered, When it's spring, when it's my birthday, that's when I like to think of what I will do new and differently. That year was Mom's sixtieth. She turned a big page in her life:

Survived breast cancer, a mastectomy, fifteen years.
Survived bladder cancer, radical experimental treatment, five years.
Stabilized on lithium, an effective drug for bipolar disease, one year.

She had lived through so much and she had so much yet to live for. Another thirty-four years. So much yet to come.

Now it was my turn. My sixtieth—a new page, a new year, a new decade, beginning a new book.

I remembered a much earlier birthday. My thirtieth was coming up and I was complaining to Mom how much I didn't want to turn thirty. She said, Why don't you just celebrate your twenty-ninth birthday every year? We can celebrate together—our shared annual twenty-ninth spring birthday party. The only limitation is that, when your oldest daughter is about to turn thirty, you'll have to celebrate your real birthday from then on.

Our daughter would be thirty in the fall. According to Mom's tradition, I would have to celebrate my real age, turning sixty, this year. However, our oldest was already complaining about turning thirty.

Mom, it sounds so old.

Why don't you adopt our annual twenty-ninth birthday idea? I suggested.

Yes. I like it, she said.

But you have to agree to the time-limiting factor, I reminded her. When your firstborn turns thirty you have to celebrate your real age unless you can negotiate a new agreement.

Sure and you'll be ninety, Mom, she teased.

I thought, I sincerely hope I'm around to see what happens. But I'm off the hook. No sixtieth party for me. My daughter and I will celebrate our shared twenty-ninth birthday together this year and carry on Mom's twenty-nine forever birthday tradition.

49

May Day, the day after my birthday. The morning of the Hike for the Hospice. It was bright and sunny, as my counselor had promised. Not overly hot. Walking the ten kilometers won't be much of a challenge, I thought, relieved. As I neared the hospice, I could hear a jazz band, excited voices, clapping and calls of welcome. There were families with strollers and infant backpacks, kids on bikes and dogs on their leashes. A banner and balloons arched colorfully over the front entrance. Volunteers in lime green T-shirts pointed to the registration desk, Pick up a white T-shirt at that table. Coffee and doughnuts are over there under the trees down by the water.

I wanted to turn and run away. I didn't like crowds at the best of times. Everyone seemed so jolly. I worried, Will someone ask me why I'm here? Will I have to say my Mom died? I come here for counseling. Just as I was turning away my grief counselor spotted me.

Hello. Come over here. Meet my team members. She hugged me and introduced me to a mother and her daughter. The little girl held up a photo of a handsome young man. It's my dad. He died last year. She said it so calmly and matter of factly. Tears filled my eyes hidden behind my sunglasses.

She said, I'm going to put my photo up on the memory tree over there. She turned to point to the big glass window at the back of the building that looked out on the garden and the river. See where the others are taping up photos onto the paper outline of a tree? Do you want to come? Who died in your family?

My Mom, I whispered.

Did you bring her photo?

I shook my head. I didn't know that's what I was supposed to do.

That's okay. They have cut-out green leaves you can write your Mom's name on. Do you want to do that now? Mom and I are just going over there.

She took my hand. I wondered, How can she be so brave?

I went with her and wrote "Mom" on a green paper leaf and taped it up on the tree beside her dad's photo.

I walked with the crowd, on my own, everyone chatting around me. I was a bit lonely but I knew I was not alone.

50

It was late spring and unseasonably cold, but it would soon be cottage time again. How I longed for that escape into the peacefulness of nature. Despite my positive conversations with my counselor I continued to be frustrated by all the unanswered questions I wished I'd asked Mom. How could you be accepting of your life when it seemed to me it was full of pain and incapacity? How could you be cheerful each day when I visited you? What did you think about death and life after? Maybe I asked you all those questions. Maybe you answered me. Maybe I was not ready then to understand what you told me.

Finally it was warm enough for a cottage weekend. I felt Mom's presence particularly strong when I was there. I walked in the forest looking for signs of early wildflowers. I smelled the muddy patches on the front lawn where a snowmobiler had left deep ruts when he drove across our property too late in the season after most of the snow had melted. I heard the northward flying geese.

Inside the cottage, it was damp and musty. I opened the windows to air it out. I wandered from room to room.

Everything was as we had left it at the end of last season: after Thanksgiving, before Remembrance Day. I picked up a book a friend had given me. It was Eckhart Tolle's *A New Earth*. I began to read it last summer but it didn't resonate with me then. So I left it behind. It seemed too philosophical. My mourning was very intense and internal at that time and I couldn't see beyond myself and my own painful experiences.

I took the book outside into the sunshine. I started reading where I had left off. What the author proposed is that I must come to acknowledge and value who I am as a conscious being above and beyond my understanding of myself as a mere physical entity. And if I am able to achieve this higher-level perception, I will recognize my conscious formless self as the essence of my self-identity, when I lose my beauty and my body grows old and weak and frail. I will comprehend that it is more important than my physical state. A few pages later he added the idea that I can find pure joy, a heaven-on-earth state, if I accept my conscious being, rather than my physical self, as the totality of who I am.[4]

I reconsidered Tolle's concepts. His words were giving me new insights into how I believed Mom had perceived her life, especially when she grew frail and incapacitated. But how had she come to know these things? How had she discovered this wisdom? Had she achieved this sense of peace and joy by letting go of things? She left her parents and her country of birth and the horrors of the war and immigrated here. She and Dad sold our family home with all its memories of our growing up and moved to a small apartment. She moved out of that apartment to a retirement home after Dad died when she could no longer manage on her own. She gave my brother and me most of her possessions. She kept her books, her journals and her letters but that was all. Had she consciously decided to give up all her belongings or were they never really important to her?

At the end of her life had her deep and profound faith enabled her to reach the state of peacefulness and inner joy that Tolle speaks of—a state he believed could be attained here on earth, if we could open our consciousness and free ourselves of our physical and material needs and wants?

Do I believe this? I asked myself. Can I? What do I believe? Want to believe? These are such difficult questions to wrestle with.

51

My mother is dead.
I'm no longer a daughter.
Then who am I now?
Loss of a role.

Rebuild my life.
Who will I become?
No longer a daughter.
Mom passed away.

Celebrate
I am a mother
With daughters.
Celebrate
Our continuity.
Mother's Day
Renewal.

52

It was the end of May. I was sitting with my counselor on the faded white wooden chairs in the hospice garden enjoying coffee and muffins

She asked, Tell me what you've been thinking about, what you've been reading. I know you're wrestling with big questions about the meaning of your own life in the context of your mother's passing.

You're right, I replied. I'm searching for a deeper understanding of Mom's life view and my own as well. How do I progress toward what Mom seemed to be—joyful, peaceful, despite the many crises in her life, the frustrations of old age, the loss of independence, the frailty of her body? Whenever I visited her I came into her presence, her sense of well-being, and I was the one consoled. I was supposed to be the one bringing her comfort. That was my ego—the good daughter syndrome.

I'm reading Eckhart Tolle again and trying to understand how his writing relates to what I'm going through. I picked up my copy of *A New Earth* when I was at the cottage. I didn't connect with what he was saying at first, but it's making more sense now. He writes that, if we are open to what is going on around us, life will provide us with the experiences that will be most helpful for the evolution and development of our consciousness. He says we have to trust that the experiences we are having are the right ones for us to have at that moment.[5]

I told her, I think that my connecting with you just when I was ready to open up is an example of having the right experience at the right moment. What Tolle writes makes sense emotionally. But I find it difficult to rationalize with my need to control and do everything myself to ensure the right next step occurs in my life—today, tomorrow, the future. I'm also not sure I fully understand what he means by our consciousness. Does he mean that we are a part of the unity of all humanity, that all our respective religions teach us— essentially the same thing—God, our God, your God loves you and cares for you?

Tolle's writings provide me with some new insights about Mom's death and her life and their impact on me now even if I don't fully understand what he says, I concluded. But I do know for the first time in my life that I have to be more conscious about who I am and what my life is about, is supposed to be about. I have to learn to let go of many things, such as my deep sorrow at losing Mom and move on.

I'm recognizing again the validity of my earlier reflection that if we ask questions, the big questions about the meaning of our life, especially in the context of the death of our loved one, we have to listen for potential answers from all the sources we come into contact with.

A colleague who has a weekly blog about how to network successfully wrote a post on the occasion of Stephen Covey's death. He described some of the author's key messages from his popular book, *The 7 Habits of Highly Effective People*. The blog post paraphrased Covey as saying we have the power to change ourselves, reinvent ourselves and become more balanced, more caring, more productive human beings. We should not consider ourselves to be trapped by our past or present circumstances, but rather acknowledge we are free to make new choices, which will help us reach fulfilment in our lives and leave a legacy for the future.[6]

I think this last part is particularly important. Mom left me her legacy. By her example she showed me how to live, to grow old and ultimately to die in peace. I know what my goal should be. I need to find my way to the sense of peace and love and internal radiance that Mom had and shared with everyone around her. She knew instinctively that every time we interact with others, we touch each other's life in some way. Each of us has the potential to have a positive impact on others' beliefs and behaviors. Our time on earth is short. When we pass on, what's left? What will we leave behind of value to others? What will my legacy be?

My counselor had been listening patiently to me. I think I'm babbling stuff again, I apologized. Am I making any sense?

That's quite a lot you're wrestling with, she said.

Yes. Sometimes I get too caught up in this interminable search for meaning. My dear friend whose mother died twenty years ago regularly e-mails me passages from her favorite gurus on life wisdom, Jerry and Esther Hicks. And again I'm surprised at the timeliness and rightness of what drops into my inbox from her. Yesterday she sent me a passage from one of their recent workshops that encourages me to experience my daily life in a spirit of fun and acceptance; that life is good and unfolding as it should; that life will never be perfect or complete because that's not possible or to be expected. Enjoy this moment, they say, and trust that whatever is happening is just what should be happening right now.[7]

It sounds so easy but I resist this concept that we should just take life as it comes. I want to believe I'm in control of what happens. But perhaps this ability to accept what life dictates is what helped Mom deal with all the ups and downs she faced. One of Mom's life lessons to me.

53

I joined a writers' circle at the beginning of June. At one of
our workshops my colleagues told me about an upcoming
writers' festival. I went with them to hear Wade Davis read
from his book *The Wayfinders*. He does anthropologic research
on remote civilizations.[8] After his presentation I asked him to
autograph my copy of his book. Please write: To my dear
daughter, enjoy your awesome adventure this summer, love
from your mom.

He asked me, Where is she going?

Sea kayaking in July along the Inner Passage off the British
Columbia coast from the northern tip of Vancouver Island to
the southern border of Alaska. On her thirty-five day journey
she has arranged to meet with the Haida watchmen to learn
how the coastal Aboriginal communities are banding together
to protect their ancient homeland from environmental damage.

I've been there, he said. It's a wild and beautiful place.

Yes. I know. Your writing about the Haida people is one of the
stories that attracted me to your book. I'm also intrigued by
the passage where you write of the Aboriginal clan leader who

is able to converse with his father's spirit as he hears his voice coming out of the flames of the campfire.

What a comfort to have that spiritual link, I said to the author, to have that contact with deceased loved ones; that belief in the continuity of the ongoing life spirit from before birth, through life, encompassing death, and moving forward and back unbounded by time and space. Our culture provides no traditions and no rituals for conversing with those who have gone before us, of seeking comfort in an ongoing dialogue with our ancestors. In fact we'd be considered somewhat demented to claim we were having conversations with the dead.

Still, I miss that possibility, I told him. I would like to believe that somehow I could talk with Mom and she with me. I'm longing to experience that sense of ongoing connection, support and comfort, but it doesn't seem to be happening yet.

54

I received an e-mail from a friend I haven't heard from in a long time. She wrote, Some years ago I came across a book of Celtic wisdom by John O'Donohue, titled *Anam Cara*.[9] I thought you might enjoy one of the blessings. May it serve to inspire you as it has me and bring you strength, courage and joy! Insert the words—Great Spirit, Universe, Mother Earth, or whatever suits, if God doesn't work for you.

The poem she sent encouraged me to remember I am a part of the natural cycle of the universe and therefore I should never feel alone. It concluded by assuring me I have a special destiny here, and that in my life there is something beautiful, good and eternal happening.

I marveled, My friend doesn't even know Mom has died, but she is thinking of me and sends this message to comfort me and remind me I'm not alone. I've heard it said, if I open my eyes and my ears to the world around me, I will find the answer I'm searching for. So often I sense it might be right there and I just don't see it. I'm not open to it.

Perhaps we do have a way to connect with some other level of consciousness. Perhaps we need to open ourselves to hearing and seeing what is around us, to be receptive to the answers that are out there. Perhaps they come in the form of a thoughtful word from a friend, a memory shared, a timely phone call, or an e-mail out of the blue to remind us we are remembered. There is, of course, the risk that the communication is simply coincidental and that we are foolish to put too much faith in its message. But, on the other hand, maybe we just need to trust ourselves and acknowledge that what we are thinking or doing is what is best.

I remembered the stained glass window in our church with the inscription: Seek and you will find, ask and you will be answered, knock and the door will be opened. I never understood this passage. I always thought, That's a nice concept but how can it be? As I sat there looking at the window a few Sundays ago, it came to me that this is the same idea I've been thinking about. I have to articulate the right question to find the answer I'm searching for. I have to know what my problem is and what I need to find a solution. I have to be conscious of what I'm searching for. Then, perhaps, if I listen actively, I might hear the advice, I might see the opportunities, I might understand what I'm learning. Maybe the answers are out there waiting for me to hear them, see them and acknowledge them. But I'm not sure.

55

Summer was coming. I needed to get in shape for the swimming and kayaking I enjoy so much. I'd stopped my regular exercise program last fall. I'd lost my sense of discipline and focus on my physical well-being as I put all my energy into wrestling with my troubled thoughts and feelings.

I decided to try yoga again. When I'd taken it up a few years ago before Mom died, I'd found it helped me pay attention to my body and my inner voice. To listen and be aware of what I was feeling internally and externally. My body needed that now especially.

In early spring I'd gone to a charity event where I met a neighbor who told me she had recently joined a yoga school. The space sounded attractive. Light and spacious, she said, and within easy walking distance of where we live. You should try it, she'd encouraged me. But I tossed the brochure she gave me into a box on my desk and went on with things as they were.

Since Mom died I'd had pain in my right heel, plantar fasciitis, so severe sometimes that I couldn't walk more than a few blocks without significant discomfort. I was a walker, jogger and hiker, so this constraint on my activities had been very frustrating. I had tried to gain some relief: foot doctor, painkillers, physiotherapy, exercises, X-ray, bone scan, orthotics. Nothing was helping. I felt that somehow I'd tied my physical pain to my emotional pain over the loss of Mom, so I had given in to the idea that this pain was never going to go away, just as I had done with my emotional pain.

I was cleaning off my desk when I came across the brochure about the yoga classes. I looked through it again and thought to myself, I know this may be just a coincidence, but I've been observing that sometimes an answer to my needs is presented to me and I need to be open to the possibility of a solution. I felt that way about finding the yoga brochure. I was suffering severe pain in my heel. Nothing was working. I trusted my neighbor's opinion. She said the classes were good. Why not try it? So I checked the yoga center's website and picked a Monday morning time slot to meet the teacher and try out a class.

Before the yoga class, the teacher read from the sutras of Patanjali: "Mistaking the transient for the permanent, the impure for the pure, pain for pleasure and that which is not the self for the self. All this is called lack of spiritual knowledge."10

In the moment of stillness after her reading, I was conscious of something new I needed to hear. I became aware that I perceived both the emotional and physical pain of my grief to be a permanent state.

I'd been trying to move forward out of my closed-in, agonizing sense of loss into a new state where I could accept that life moved on. But I kept falling back to my old thoughts: this pain is not going away no matter what you tell me, no matter what I read.

After the yoga class, I asked the teacher if she could suggest some movements I could do to relieve the pain in my heel.

Stand there, she said, and I'll have a look. I see that each leg is positioned very differently. One knee is straight, the other is twisted in. One foot is placed evenly flat on the floor, the other turns outward onto the edge of your foot where you feel the pain in your heel. I will suggest some exercises that will help you. Slowly your strong leg and foot will teach your misaligned leg and foot how to stand correctly. You will help yourself by being aware of what is out of balance and by moving consciously into balance again. This will take time. But this is a first step.

It seemed to me that what I was trying to achieve physically was also what I was trying to achieve mentally and emotionally. My counselor was helping me to do that: externalize my feelings of sorrow and acknowledge that my deep grief was out of balance; that in time I would accept I would always mourn Mom. But I would also begin to experience the happy times we had shared, the positive aspects of her life, the legacy she'd left me.

56

I spent a relaxing July at the cottage. During my time there I began to sense a distinct shift in my outlook. Sixteen months after Mom's passing I no longer thought of myself as being on my grief journey but rather as being in a new creative space in which I was exploring how I could communicate what I'd experienced, and how I was progressing and changing along the way.

At the beginning of August my husband and I returned to the city and I settled into my routine of work, volunteering, going to counseling and exercise. At my yoga class the first week I was back the teacher described the benefits of healing touch therapy. She said it was an energy-based approach to health and healing that uses touch to influence the human energy system. She said the goal is to restore harmony and balance in the energy system so that we are in a position to self-heal. That's what I was trying to do, find balance and harmony in my life. I decided to give it a try.

I arrived at the therapist's office. She settled me into a comfortable chair. I didn't know what to expect but I was not apprehensive. It was a hot summer morning. I took off my sandals and felt the cool tiles under my feet. I closed my eyes. I sensed her presence around me. A light touch on my knees, on my shoulders. I let my mind slip away somewhere else for a while. I was not conscious of what I was thinking. I was aware I wasn't sleeping but I felt as if I were dreaming. Dreaming but without images. I hoped I might see Mom or perhaps hear her voice, but no. Just this feeling of well-being. Waiting perhaps for what was to come next in my life.

After our session, the therapist said, I felt a great calm within you. Water flowing among rocks. I feel replenished, I said, and very peaceful and reassured that I'm on the right track. I thanked her and returned home, thinking my journey continues toward renewal and hopefulness.

I remembered my best friend encouraging me to be more aware of the present moment and how I feel, not to always be thinking about the past and what is over and gone. Focus on the now she keeps reminding me. That is where your life is happening. Your life is right now.

57

How are you? my counselor greeted me.

That's such a simple question, I replied. You know how hard it used to be for me to answer it honestly when anyone asked. I would just say, I'm fine. Nothing more because I didn't want to tear up and blurt out, I feel awful. My Mom died. I would angrily say to myself, I know you're asking me the standard how are you, but I really don't want to know if you're still feeling sad and lonely about losing your mother version of the question. And I would feel justified in not answering. But I'm much better now at responding openly no matter who asks. And I know you always expect a genuine and substantive answer.

You're right, she smiled. You really are going to have to give me a good answer. We haven't seen each other since the end of June and now it's almost September. How did you enjoy the healing touch therapy? What have you been thinking about? What have you been learning about coming to terms with the loss of your mother?

I answered, I'm listening more attentively and being more observant of what is going on around me. I'm actively searching for answers to all the unasked and unanswered questions I had for Mom. How could you cope with all your grief and loss? How could you not be angry and frustrated when you had to bear so much pain? How could you continue to be joyful and in the end peaceful about your life as death was nearing?

For the first year after Mom's death I shouted those questions despairingly into the silent void of my unconsciousness and buried myself in my grief. But now I want to ask, What can I learn from what you experienced Mom? How can I discover what you knew, about death and loss, joy and life, that brought you so much peace? How can I apply what I'm coming to understand about your life and your death to my life, my own mortality?

I turned to my counselor, You help me by asking questions I'm compelled to answer and thereby to express my thoughts and feelings out loud so I can hear them and acknowledge what is going on in my head and in my heart. I'm making progress understanding the impact of Mom's death on my life. Talking about her and me and our relationship helps me get it all out in the open in a way I could never do on my own.

You know I've been struggling with these questions for a while now, trying to come to terms with Mom's death, my own grief journey, and how to consciously move forward. The big question remains, How do I grow beyond my present state to the next stage of my life? During my time away at the cottage I felt I was nearing a new more hopeful place in my life, but I'm not there yet.

58

I first heard about post traumatic growth last spring on a radio program. The idea caught my attention. I did some reading on the subject but I found the research outcomes contradictory. I recently came across the notes I'd made. Reading through them I thought, I'm more ready now to grapple with the concept and figure out how it might help me understand Mom's approach to life.

I was also trying to settle on the right word to describe the next stage of my journey beyond mourning. I didn't like the frequently used term *grief recovery*. I didn't consider it meaningful when applied to grieving. To me the phrase suggested being able to go back to the way things were and I was certain that was not possible. Mom had passed on and the wonderful times we spent together would never come back. No one and no experience in my life now or in the future would replace that.

I preferred the word *renewal*: "to renew, make new again." Not very helpful, but the dictionary offered *replenish* as a synonym: "to refill or make complete again," replenish the larder; "to inspire or nourish," the music will nourish my weary soul. More hopeful.

As the months passed I'd grown more aware of what my own needs were and how to try to satisfy them, not in an entirely selfish way, but because I had to look after myself so I could look after my loved ones. And I had to move forward with my life, find a new role and create my own legacy. My counselor helped me understand how important it was to articulate my needs and satisfy them. As I tried to come to terms with Mom's death and my own mortality, I was learning to think differently about my life. I was ready for deeper self-exploration. I would need to change and grow if I wanted to move to a new stage, to move forward on the journey of life, beyond this present state of mourning.

I did more reading on post traumatic growth. There were many articles on the subject. Some researchers endorsed the concept and others claimed to have proven it was not a widespread experience. But generally there was agreement that post traumatic growth was not a return to baseline after a period of suffering and, therefore, not a state of recovery, as in grief recovery.

The writings, which supported my experiences with grieving, described post traumatic growth as a positive change in some people, which came about as a result of struggling with highly stressful life circumstances that significantly challenge an individual's resilience, capacity to adapt and ability to make sense of the world.[11]

Perhaps the very fact of getting through an extremely difficult life experience creates a sense of having grown to meet the challenges one had to face.

Other research suggested that the impression of positive change growing out of a deeply traumatic life experience might represent a defensive illusion. When people were confronted by a trauma or loss, they often struggled to understand why the event happened and tried to make sense out of the tragedy. Given all that might have been lost following a trauma, survivors might want to convince themselves that something good had come out of it: "Out of loss there is gain."[12]

These descriptions of post traumatic growth helped me understand how Mom might have coped with her deep sadness at leaving her homeland and her elderly parents who were mourning the loss of their three sons killed in the war. How she survived all those illnesses, physical and mental, and the frailties of old age, and how she could still be cheerful and ultimately at peace with herself. Perhaps that overworked phrase "what doesn't kill you makes you strong" had some basis in fact. Perhaps it was Mom's own resilience and adaptive nature that helped her overcome those terrible losses in her life and move beyond her grief and suffering.

I reflected, If there is one word that describes Mom, it would be resilient. The literature about post traumatic growth uses these words: *resilient, resilience,* to refer to the ability to recover from trauma or crisis. Maybe she drew on her deep spiritual roots to enable her to believe that some good had to come out of all she suffered. Either way, the term puts some logic into what I have found so hard to understand for so long.

Claudia Chowaniec

I recently read a newspaper article, "God as Drug." Rather an eye-catching title, I thought. It examined research that seemed to indicate that religious belief takes the sting out of living. It said that a new Canadian study, published in *Psychological Science*, provided a clue as to why religious people tended to lead longer lives and enjoy better physical and mental health. It established that a belief in God worked much like an anti-anxiety drug, creating a buffer against defensive or distressing reactions to life's crises and traumas.[13]

I thought this was also part of the answer to my questioning. Mom was a deeply religious person. I knew she had found great comfort in reading her Bible every day as well as religious stories and texts. She was always trying to give me her books to read but I didn't derive any comfort from them. Why was that? I was often angry at all she had to suffer—deaths, diseases, frailty and loneliness. Then there was my terrible guilt that I could not help her more. And also my anger that she hadn't always been there for me when I needed her, especially when I was a young teenager and she was in the psychiatric hospital.

Speaking with friends who have lost loved ones, and reading the comments I received on my blog from individuals trying to cope with their own grief, showed me how each of us responds in very different ways to the shock of death and the overwhelming sadness that follows. For me, I could recall only two stages in my mourning: the first ten months or so when I experienced a constant chaos of emotions—deep sadness, guilt, emptiness, sleeplessness—and now, more than a year after

268

Mom's death, an emerging sense of arriving at a new state I was calling *renewal*, an improvement in the way I felt that was profound. The deep sorrow was fading and the happier memories of what we shared were rising to the surface, along with the desire to tell Mom's story, her legacy to me.

It was also important to me that what I was reading, for example, the research on post traumatic growth was attesting to my own experiences and helping me sort through some possible explanations for Mom's profound resilience and her life-affirming view on what she'd experienced.

59

I was rereading Mom's stories, which I had written down in my journal before she died. They reminded me that while my memories of Mom focused on the personal tragedies and medical traumas she endured when I was growing up with my brother in the relative post-World War Two calm of small-town Canada, there were so many other parts to Mom's life. My fascination with her stories and the reason I had to write them down was not only that they seemed to bring her pleasure when I read them back to her, but also that they represented a whole different aspect of the person I knew as Mom. In her stories, particularly the ones set during and just after the war, she was young, attractive, adventuresome, independent and self-reliant. Maybe those early experiences gave her the strength and courage to carry on and be a survivor throughout her difficult life.

I came to realize that Mom must have had a strong will and immense resilience to overcome the hardships she faced with such endurance and courage. She knew these things intuitively, I supposed, but it was only now that I began to truly understand who she was and what her life and her death meant to me. This is her story, I reflected, her legacy, and it continues to be an inspiration to me. Remembering to remember all this has helped me come to terms with her death and her absence from my life. I am acknowledging all she gave me, taught me, left with me. I hope that in my own life I can match her courage and strength and belief.

60

It was early October, one of my favorite times of the year. Days still warm. Nights cool. Trees turning scarlet, gold, bronze. My counselor greeted me, You know, you've come a long way since our first get-together ten months ago and I don't think you need our regular sessions any more. What do you think?

I agreed. You've helped me talk about Mom, what she suffered, and my mourning for her, and you've helped me recall happy memories. Mom's homemade cakes for every celebratory occasion. We've shared many events here at the hospice— Valentine's, Mother's Day and your charity walk on my sixtieth birthday and my promise to join your team again next year.

My counselor reassured me, You can call me anytime, especially if you're having a hard time getting through the upcoming holidays. It won't be long before it's Thanksgiving and Christmas again. I'd also like to ask you, she continued, if you would talk to the second-year medical students taking the course in palliative medicine. The hospice director hosts an annual session on the topic and invites guest speakers to describe their personal experiences of being with a loved one who is dying, and suffering through grief and loss.

It's not until next April, she explained. I suggested you would be an excellent speaker. You've told me about your frustrations dealing with the medical staff when your mother was dying and how you found palliative care services for her. You've learned to express your thoughts and feelings and you've said yourself you think you're making progress in dealing with your grief and moving toward a new stage of renewal. Would you be prepared to do this?

Yes, I answered without hesitation. It's been my goal for a while now to share my story with the hope that what I've been through will help others feel less alone with their grief and know that time does heal, even if it takes an awful long time.

I can look back from this moment of new hopefulness and see the steps in my journey, when I made a leap ahead and when I slipped down again into my sorrow and loneliness. I remember the intense remorseless pain of my grief. The big empty hole in my life that I thought could never be filled.

There is a space I hold inside me. A space filled with great joy. And such great sadness. I remember Mom. Our space shared, our time together. I know now I could not have had the one without the other.

Dying
Death
Grief
Loss
My mother is dead.

Comfort
Remembering
Her
Her legacy
Who she was.

I feel freer. More able to be alive to this moment. To this life. My life. Mom is constantly present within me. I see a photo of our girls being silly and I'm sharing it with Mom and we're smiling together. I hear myself laughing and Mom saying, Oh yes. Laugh. I love to hear you. It reminds me of my father's laugh. I touch a piece of dark green silk interwoven with patterns of silver thread and I know how delighted she would be to hold it too. The burden of my grief is lighter. The happy memories are coming to the forefront. Sunlight overshadows the mourning.

I am in a new place in my life where the immense sadness is slowly receding and I'm learning that in time, time heals.

61

I was planning a trip to San Francisco. I would arrive on
November 1 and meet my two daughters there. The following
day we would join several thousand other celebrants and walk
together in the annual parade through the Mission District.
We would be accompanied by brass bands, jazz ensembles,
choirs, street entertainers, and dancers. We would all be there
to celebrate All Souls Day—*La Dia de los Muertos*, a very old
tradition for honoring the dead.

I'd celebrated All Souls with family members and friends many
years ago in Europe. We marked the occasion by going to the
cemetery, placing candles on the tombs of deceased loved
ones, and praying for the dead and for the living too.

Now I wanted to relive this experience with my daughters by
honoring Mom's passing. I explained to them that the event in
San Francisco was based on an ancient Mesoamerican
celebration of the cycle of life and death, which began long
before Europeans landed in the Americas. When the Spanish
arrived they linked the rituals of the indigenous people to the
Catholic Feast of All Souls. The gods and goddesses of the
natural world were replaced by the Virgin Mary, the Trinity
and the saints.

People from all cultures would participate, carrying candles and photos of family members who had died. Nearly everyone would paint their face white, some with eerie death heads, skulls with black eyes, and others would decorate their cheeks with vibrant floral designs in a uniquely San Francisco flower-child style.

My daughters and I checked out *La Dia de los Muertos* website that showed how to apply traditional white face patterns. We helped each other with our makeup creating our own designs.

I wanted to participate in this walk with my daughters through the streets at night. I wanted to hold my candle and my photo of Mom. I wanted to share my mourning with all the people who would be walking with me in memory of their loved ones who had passed on. I was hoping this experience of collective public mourning would help me let go a little more of my suffering the loss of Mom.

Day of the Dead
Night of the Dead
Dia de los Muertos
In the Latino heart
of San Francisco
we move easily
into the crowd
walking slowly
walking solemnly
from the Mission
de la Rosa
arm in arm

my daughters and I
carrying our memories
alone together
sorrow joy life death
Mom Grandmother
my daughters and I
arm in arm
walking quietly
walking reverently
holding our candles
each with our thoughts
together with thousands
flickering candles in the
balmy November night.
Whose gentle face is this
remembered in your photo?
Your loss your grief
our loss our grief
we share our memories
and find solace together
unexpectedly comforting
here among strangers
in a crowd of thousands
mourning together
alone with our memories
sharing this experience
walking together
to the steady beat
of a lone drum.

Day of the Dead
Night of the Dead
Dia de los Muertos
Face painted white
Eye hollows black
Lips vibrant red
White face, not skull.
Day of the Dead
Night of the Dead
Dia de los Muertos
We turn a corner and meet a chaos of sound and
movement. White-clothed musicians raise their instruments.
Bright bold jazz fills the soft darkness of flickering candlelight.
Stilt walkers in frenzied gyrations move through our
crowd. Flamenco dancers swirl in wide ruffled skirts, their
partners in brilliant red vests and broad black-brimmed hats.
Day of the Dead
Night of the Dead
Dia de los Muertos
Here is the Park
our gathering place
shrines to loved ones
red flickering candles
photos and marigold
wreaths hung in trees
ancient mythical pagan
traditions now catholic
our common act of mourning.

There is a ribbon stretched between two trees crowded with
notes pegged to the line.
Messages sent to loved ones. Paper and a pencil offered.
Write. Remember them.
We will leave our candles
here join them with others
in a circle of marigolds
Mom planted each spring in her
garden we choose this place
we set down our candles
we leave them here
pray silently a moment and
turn away from the crowds.
Day of the Dead
Night of the Dead
Dia de los Muertos
Walking home
alone with our thoughts
together with our memories
arm in arm
my daughters and I.

Epilogue

My story that began with such deep sorrow has metamorphosed into a new stage in the continuity of my life.

Christmas passed quietly. Then January and February. At the end of March my counselor and I met to review my presentation to the second-year medical students in the palliative medicine program.

April 6. Two years and four days after Mom died. I was standing beside a small desk at the front of the university lecture hall holding my notes tightly and trying to keep my hands from shaking. I worried, Can I do this or will I break down in tears? I began slowly, I would like to speak with you about grief, what I experienced as my mother was dying, and then her death, almost two years ago. This is the first time I've spoken in public about my feelings then and now, so I'm finding it a bit difficult. But I do want to tell you my story. You are about to make the transition from your classroom to the practical world of hospitals and clinics. You will be working directly with all kinds of people—practitioners and patients. You will be dealing with real-life situations and, perhaps for the first time, with death.

My voice grew stronger. It was time to tell my story, to describe the stages of my mourning, what I suffered, what it was like dealing with the medical team, how lacking in compassion they often seemed, how little they knew about palliative care in the community.

This was the core of my message to these young people beginning their medical careers. Be open to the opportunities to show compassion. Recognize that life and death should be treated as a continuum. Communicate empathetically with your patients who are dying and with their families. Acknowledge that you are there not only to find a cure and save lives but also to ease the path toward dying. Learn all you can about palliative medicine even if it is not your chosen field of practice.

I made it through. I sat down. The students applauded. Many asked thoughtful questions and listened respectfully to my replies.

Following this lecture I coauthored an article for the *Canadian Medical Association Journal* titled, "Conversations on Dying: Giving a Family Member the Last Word." I wrote about the need for better and more timely communication with the dying and their families to ensure they have clear information on what is happening and, in particular, about the palliative care resources in their community.[14]

A young woman who launched the Canadian Virtual Hospice website saw the article and asked me to be a regular contributor to the site. Members of her team respond to readers' on-line comments and initiate subject threads relevant to palliative care and experiencing the death of a loved one.[15]

I've developed a new website: www.MemoirofMourning.com, with a link to my blog: www.GriefShared.com, to enable us to have an ongoing conversation about our experiences with grief and loss and the journey toward renewal.

In June I went to our cottage for the first time after the long cold snowy winter. I was joyful being there. I was conscious of a weight lifted from me. A weight I'd grown accustomed to. But now I felt its absence, a new lightness inside me.

It has taken me four years to work my way through my mourning. I hiked for the hospice again and saw some old friends. The little girl whose father died has grown quite tall. I hardly recognized her. I met the woman who did the same presentation as I did last year to the second-year students in palliative medicine. Our counselor took a photo—her two grads she calls us. She introduced us to the woman who has already been asked to make the presentation next year.

Why are we so eager to tell our story? We know the relief it brings us and we know sharing our stories will bring comfort to others who are mourning their loved one.

Notes

1. Sara Gruen, *Water for Elephants* (Toronto: Harper Perennial, 2006).

2. Lhasa de Sela, "I Come In," *Ottawa Citizen* (January 2010.) She was a Montreal singer and song writer who died at the age of thirty-seven after battling breast cancer.

3. Cindy Stelmackowich, "Cholera Shapes and Spaces Series," from an art piece titled "The Disaster Series Triptych 2007."

4. Eckhart Tolle, *A New Earth* (New York: Plume Books, 2005), p. 43.

5. Ibid., p. 51.

6. Stephen Covey, *The 7 Habits of Highly Effective People* (New York: Free Press, a division of Simon & Schuster Inc., 1989).

7. From a workshop presentation by Jerry and Esther Hicks, 20 February 2001, Tucson, AZ.

8. Wade Davis, *The Wayfinders* (Toronto: Anansi Press, 2009).

9. John O'Donohue, *Anam Cara: A Book of Celtic Wisdom* (New York: Cliff Street Books, 1997).

10. The sage, Patanjali, compiled 195 sutras (words of wisdom) in the Yoga Sutra, the guidebook to classical yoga, seventeen hundred years ago.

11. Jan Bernard and Miriam Schneider, *The True Work of Dying: A Practical and Compassionate Guide to Easing the Process of Dying* (New York: Avon Books, 1997).

12. J.H. Ellard and C.B. Wortman, *Post Traumatic Growth: Progress and Problems* (Stoney Brook, NY: SUNY, 1986); and C.G. Davis, C.B. Wortman, D.R. Lehman and R.C. Silver, *Death Studies* (Stoney Brook, NY: SUNY, 2000).

13. The article appeared in *The Globe and Mail*, March 2012 and was based on research by Michael Inzlicht and Alexa Tullett, "Reflecting on God," *Psychological Science* 21 (Aug 2011): 1184-1190.

14. Dr. Tara Tucker and Claudia Chowaniec, "Conversations on Dying: Giving a Family Member the Last Word," *Canadian Medical Association Journal* (6 March 2012): 444. It was also published on-line at: cmaj.ca (Oct 2011).

15. Colleen Young is the community manager for the Canadian Virtual Hospice website: www.virtualhospice.ca.

Acknowledgments

Love and gratitude to my dearest family to whom this book is dedicated. My husband, Adam, and my daughters, Christina and Alexandra—you encouraged me and kept me going on my sorrowful journey mourning Mom. You supported me through the difficult weeks and months that turned into four years before I was able to recognize I had reached a new phase and could acknowledge life moves on, time heals. My brother, Joh, and sister-in-law, Inez, were always there for me. My cousin, Ilina, Mom's goddaughter, shared with me in a personal and intimate way her memories of Mom and her reflections on reading *Memoir of Mourning*.

I deeply appreciate the professional guidance and friendship of Francine Beaupré, MSW, RSW, who was my grief counselor at the Hospice at May Court. She helped me unlock my deep-down hidden-away thoughts and feelings and encouraged me to tell her my stories.

I especially thank Sandra O'Neill Page who continues to e-mail and phone me with her nurturing and caring advice. You constantly remind me that our mothers are still somehow very present in our lives.

I want to thank Jean Van Loon, a remarkably talented short story writer who was the first person to professionally critique my earliest draft. JC Sulzenko, Ottawa poet, playwright and author of many delightful children's stories and poems, comforted me even as she was mourning her own mother's passing, and wisely suggested I consult a grief counselor. She was also kind enough to comment on an early draft of my manuscript.

Dr. Mary Morris, Dr. Rob Cushman and Dr. Tara Tucker empathized with my frustration at the medical profession's lack of effective communication skills to support the dying and their families. Tara, thank you also for inviting me to speak to your medical students in palliative care because you felt they needed to hear about suffering and grief from someone who is experiencing it, and for your professional advocacy in coauthoring the article in the *Canadian Medical Association Journal* (March 2012).

Colleen Young is the innovative moderator of the Canadian Virtual Hospice on-line community. I thank her for inviting me to be part of her core member team. Core members offer solace and support to those who post on the community forums seeking understanding and guidance from peers.

I heartily thank my two wise and nurturing editors, Suzanne Clores and Maggie Kast, who each in her own unique and creative way provided me with very different and equally valuable insights into my writing. Together they informed my writing approach and helped shape my drafts from the beginning. I thank Kim Lymburner, my friend and advisor, for helping me connect with Maggie and Suzanne.

Keef Ward is the creative web designer who collaborated with me to develop both my site: www.MemoirOfMourning.com and my blog: www.SharingGrief.com. The book cover is based on the beautiful photo he took the Christmas before Mom passed on. He is also helping me market my book utilizing innovative web-based business practices.

With precision and patience, Evelyn Budd designed my book and Eleanor Sawyer copyedited my manuscript. I'm grateful for their experience. McEvoy Galbreath continues to advise me on self-publishing and marketing.

I would like to thank all the staff members of the Colonel By Retirement Residence. You cared for Mom with compassion for the nine years she was a resident. And in particular you provided excellent palliative care in the last weeks of her life.

I would like to thank my dear friends, colleagues and neighbors who read my manuscript in its many drafts and provided me with helpful comments. You thought I had something to say that would comfort others who are experiencing sorrow and loneliness in the passing of their own loved one. Many of you told me your own stories of loss. I deeply value your sharing your experiences with me.

About the Author

Claudia Chowaniec, PhD, CMC, is a published author, poet and facilitator. She is actively engaged in her community as a volunteer and board member, past and present, of organizations, including the Ottawa Art Gallery, YM-YWCA, Chamber of Commerce, National Capital Commission and the Canadian Museum of Nature, where she chaired a successful national fundraising campaign.

She coauthored an article for the *Canadian Medical Association Journal* titled, "Conversations on Dying: Giving a Family Member the Last Word" (March 2012). She wrote about the need for better and more timely communication with the dying and their families to ensure they have clear information about what is happening and, in particular, about the palliative care resources in their community.

Claudia contributes regularly to the Canadian Virtual Hospice website as a member of the team of writers who respond to readers' on-line comments and questions and initiate new subject threads relevant to palliative care and end-of-life experiences. She develops training programs for hospice volunteers and palliative care support workers.

Claudia is also President of Precept Consulting and has more than thirty years experience in Canada and the United States as an advisor, coach and consultant in the fields of strategic, business and human resource planning, management development, organization restructuring and board governance. She works with organizations, their boards and staff to guide their strategic planning and to help implement improvements and changes required to meet future goals.

She has written numerous articles on facilitating large group change and strategic planning in the corporate, public and not-for-profit communities.

Claudia was educated at Queen's University and York University and holds a PhD from the University of Leeds in Great Britain. She taught at Carleton University and served as Senior Research Fellow at the Centre on Governance at the University of Ottawa.

Please visit her blog at www.SharingGrief.com and her website at www.MemoirOfMourning.com.